LIBRARY
PLANTING FIELDS FOUNDATION

Forever Flowers

REJEAN METZLER

Charles Scribner's Sons   New York

Copyright © 1972 Rejean Metzler

This book published simultaneously in the
United States of America and in Canada —
Copyright under the Berne Convention.

All rights reserved. No part of this book
may be reproduced in any form without the
permission of Charles Scribner's Sons.

A–10.72 (Q)

Printed in the United States of America
Library of Congress Catalog Card Number 72–37215
SBN 684—12755—5 (Trade cloth)

To my husband,

Maurice,

whose humorous tolerance and wisdom
makes it possible for me to live this charmed life

The Roxbury-Bridgewater Garden Club
is accredited by the
Federated Garden Clubs of Connecticut as a
Teaching Team for Holiday Decoration
Designs pictured are the work of club members

PHOTOGRAPHS BY GREG SHARP
Sketches by Barbara Goodspeed

THE DESIGNS IN THIS BOOK ARE THE WORK OF
THESE ROXBURY-BRIDGEWATER GARDEN CLUB MEMBERS

*Mrs. Stuart Abseck
*Mrs. Joseph Adams
 Miss Anne Brownell
 Mrs. Donald S. Campbell
*Mrs. Theodore Chajka
*Mrs. Theodore Demko
 Mrs. Nicholas DeVries
 Mrs. John Dow
 Mrs. Bernice Everett
*Mrs. Edward H. Fuller
 Miss Janet Gribbon
 Mrs. James H. Hand
*Mrs. Harold Heap
*Mrs. Howard C. Hopkins
 Mrs. Walter O. Howard
*Mrs. Murray D. Jackson
 Mrs. Albert Jeffcoat
 Mrs. J. R. Kavasch
*Mrs. Weston C. Knight
*Mrs. Martin E. Kornbluth
*Mrs. Milton E. MacEslin
 Mrs. B. J. Mattuck
 Mrs. William C. Meintzer
*Mrs. Maurice W. Metzler, Jr.
*Mrs. William A. Moore

 Mrs. Robert Munson
 Mrs. Earl E. Murdock
*Mrs. Gustav T. Muth
 Mrs. Charles Meier
 Mrs. Charles M. Northrup
 Mrs. Herbert D. Olson
*Mrs. Thomas P. Peardon
*Mrs. Stewart M. Pratt
 Mrs. Philip D. Richmond
*Mrs. Richard H. Roberts
 Mrs. Lloyd Robertson
*Mrs. Peter Rossiter
 Mrs. W. Lorne Scovil
*Mrs. Warren M. Seaman
*Mrs. Norman G. Shidle
 Mrs. Walter Skor
 Miss Rebecca Stackhouse
*Mrs. Jared Synnestvedt
 Mrs. Anthony P. Tedesco
 Mrs. Walter Van Lenten
*Miss Clara Velting
 Mrs. John P. Waters
*Mrs. C. Edward Wells
*Mrs. Helen Whittles
*Mrs. Eugene Wright, Jr.

*Teachers

ACKNOWLEDGEMENTS

THANK YOU
>   to
Margaret Perry
>   who caused this book to be written
>   to
Georgette Schmidt and Weston C. Knight
>   for their knowledgeable assistance
>   to
my friends of the Roxbury-Bridgewater Garden Club
>   for their enthusiastic cooperation
>   to
Greg Sharp, Barbara Goodspeed, Barbara Fuller
>   for their excellence
>   to
Elinor Parker
>   for her trust

NO MATERIALS ON THE LIST FOR PRESERVATION OF WILD PLANTS
IN CONNECTICUT ARE USED IN THIS BOOK.
PLEASE OBSERVE YOUR STATE CONSERVATION PRACTICES

List of Color Figures

Contents

Introduction

Forever flowers are a new adventure in the world of art and nature. From the new adventure, a new term, *Climax Material,* evolves to distinguish the noble forms of the mature plant world from other media.

There are single flowers, boutonnieres, candle trims, arrangements for table and mantel, and hangings for wall or door. Simple techniques were developed for these designs, and nature lovers, artists, homemakers, civic groups, and garden club members have responded with enthusiasm to exhibits and workshops.

The materials can be found in gardens, fields, woods, and along the roadside. The time to collect them is when the first seedpod sets on the columbine in early spring, and on through the frozen days in December, when evergreens like myrtle, leucothoe, hardy ivy, and andromeda can be cut, thawed, and perpetuated in a glycerin-and-water solution.

Much of the material used in these designs, as well as tape, wire, and paint can be bought at florists' supply shops. No special training is needed. The inspiration comes with picking up a pod or leaf and looking at it with care.

Here you can turn a leaf into a flower petal or a pod into a leaf, and a spruce cone can become a miniature Christmas wreath. There is as much stimulus in this adventure as in a walk through the woods, and as much creation in store for you as there are time and materials available.

1 Supplies and Sources

Materials needed are listed with each pictured design. The places where they can be found are given below. Many large cities have florists' supply shops and most of the mechanical aids as well as much dried material can be purchased there. A friendly electrician will have quantities of used wires. A lumberyard has heaps of scraps. With experience many new sources will occur to you.

Florists' Supply Shops

Styrofoam balls
floral spray paint
Accent spray paint
Floralescent spray paint
glitter glue
glitter dust
Floratape ½″ width
floral adhesive tape
ribbon, satin, knockout
bound wire nos. 18 & 26
spool or stick wire, nos. 19, 21, 26, 30

Hardware Stores

prepasted canvas picture hangers
Elmer's Glue-All or Sobo Glue
linoleum paste
Derusto fluorescent spray paint
plaster of Paris
assorted screw eyes
small swivels
masking tape
heavy duty stapler
sandpaper
Quickee hand cleaner

Electrical Supply Stores

bound wire nos. 10, 12, 14

Drugstores	*Also*
Coban Elastic Bandage	a pair of small pliers
absorbent cotton balls	a small sturdy pair of clippers
Q-Tips	that can cut wire, small cones
orris root and alum	a sharp knife
	a hammer and assorted nails
	scissors
	assorted needles
	nylon thread
	spring clothespins or other
	clamps

These climax materials need no special treatment and can be obtained from florists' supply shops or found in gardens and woods. Pods are best picked at maturity and allowed to dry away from the light.

Plant Seed Pods	*Tree Pods*	*Cones*
honesty	tulip	pine
Chinese lantern	gum	hemlock
iris	alder	spruce
yucca	beech	fir
sweet cicely	magnolia	cedar
lily	larch	
poppy	sandalwood	*Seed Pod Stalks*
datura	mahogany	
burdock	coconut	sensitive fern
abutilon		mustard
hosta	*Tree Leaves*	radish
mallow		coconut
wild cucumber	oak	
		Berries
Seed Spikes	*Plant Leaves*	
		rose
pokeweed	artemisia	privet
polygonum twigs	palm	euonymus
		bay

The following forms can be found in your kitchen and should be dried naturally.

Fruit Parts: Halves of orange, lime, and lemon, turned inside out. Banana skins cleaned of pulp, cut vertically in two or three strips. Mango seeds, dried and split.

Vegetable Parts: Stem and throat (calyx) end of eggplant and persimmon.

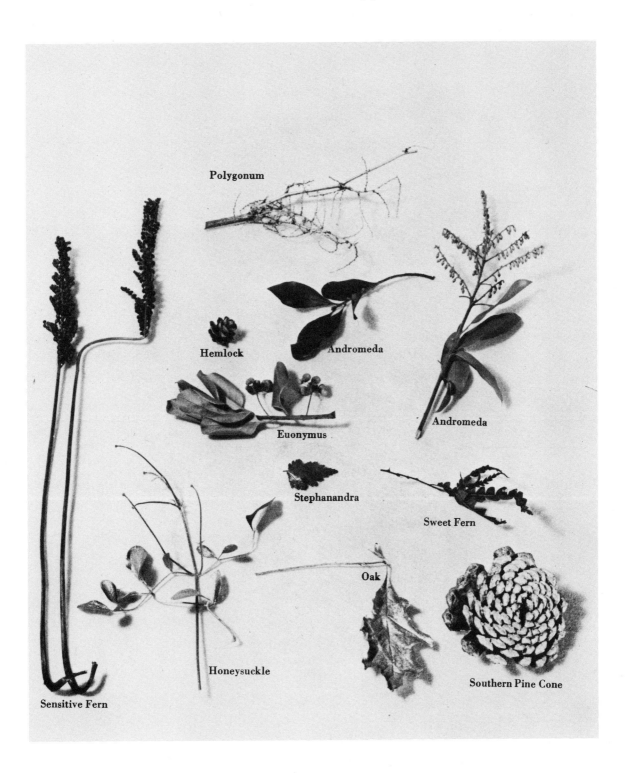

Polygonum

Hemlock

Andromeda

Andromeda

Euonymus

Stephanandra

Sweet Fern

Oak

Honeysuckle

Sensitive Fern

Southern Pine Cone

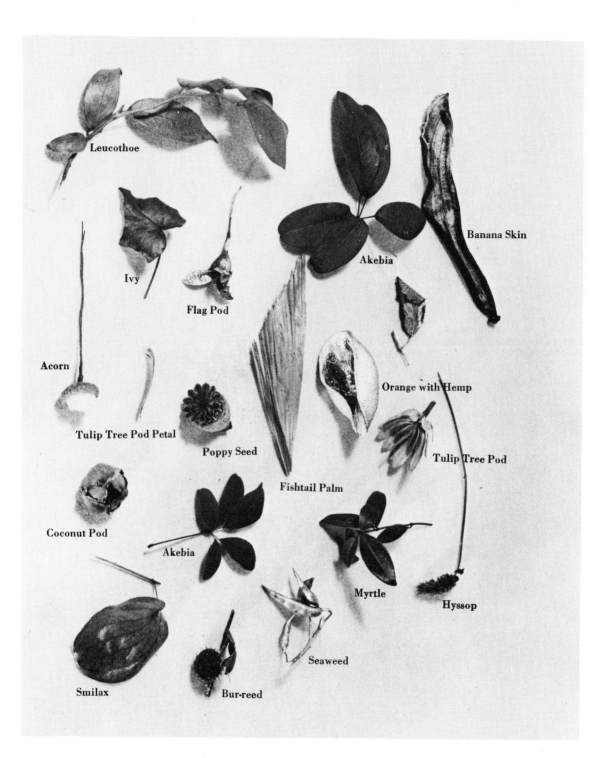

The leaves listed below are durable after being treated with glycerin. These can be found in garden or woods. Some are available from mail order sources.*

Trees	*Vines*	*Bushes*	*Plants*
beech	honeysuckle	viburnum	sweet fern
magnolia	clematis	euonymus	coltsfoot
mulberry	smilax	andromeda	spikenard
eucalyptus	ivy	leucothoe	physostegia
apple	akebia	spiraea	hyssop
pear	myrtle	bay	rubber
		rose	dracaena
		stephanandra	
		sea grape	

*Dorothy Biddle Service, 8 Broadway, Hawthorne, N.Y.
S. Hanfling and Company, 24 West 28th Street, New York, N.Y.
Pod Happy Shop, Third Avenue South, St. Petersburg, Fla.
Kervan Company, 119 West 28th Street, New York, N.Y.

2 Preserving and Decorating

1. GLYCERIN

Only hardened growth such as stiff, leathery leaves, will respond to glycerin treatment. New candidates are discovered every year, however, and you will enjoy the search.

Cut stems of fresh material under water. Let stand overnight in cold water six to eight inches deep (well supported) in container.

Woody stems and branches absorb moisture better if stems are scraped on opposite sides for three inches upward from cut end. One part glycerin to two parts water is a workable solution.

After the material is conditioned satisfactorily, transfer to a pinholder to ensure that stem ends remain upright, and place in glycerin-water solution, which need not be more than two inches deep, and in a container where you can easily check the level of the solution, since it may be rapidly absorbed in the first few days. Maintain a minimum two-inch level by adding water to the solution. The absorption period varies from a week to three weeks, heavy stems taking longer to absorb the solution than thin ones.

Ivy is one of the few leaves that keeps green; other leaves turn copper, beige, or red tones. Flower leaves are usually completed in ten days. The leaf is pliable and leathery after glycerin has been absorbed. In some cases a plant will "weep" — the glycerin seeps out through the leaf. This may be washed off with soapy water, but it is best to try again with a more hardened specimen. Any glycerin residue will spoil the next step in the design since it will leave a sticky surface and be unattractive without spray, or, if spray is used, it will not adhere evenly. Take care when removing stems from glycerin solution to cut off and discard all parts that have been in the solution. They cannot be taped or sprayed as neither paint nor paste will adhere.

2. CLEARSPRAY

Clearspray is another preservative step. It can be applied to untreated or treated material, sometimes leaving a high sheen on nonporous surfaces. It is wise to test it on a sample before using it on an entire design. Do not use as an undercoat. (See Two Flower Leucothoe, page 52, for special use in preserving.)

3. SPRAY PAINT

All the floral spray paints have preservative qualities.

A large box about one foot deep and two feet square will be useful as a work saver. This movable spray box will eliminate cleaning up as there is a certain amount of residue or "fallout" powder from the spraying procedure. If it is not possible to work outdoors an ideal place is near an exhaust fan.

A piece of tissue paper under the object you are spraying can be moved around in the spray box as a lever without touching wet surfaces or waiting for one side to dry at a time. When spraying several leaves, a small flat box serves nicely as a tray in which the leaves can be shaken, poked, and flipped with a long stick while spraying.

After thoroughly shaking the can, apply paint from a distance of eight inches, moving can constantly to avoid heavy concentrations of paint. Apply light coats two or three separate times, allowing to dry for five minutes between applications.

Floral spray paints have a soft, natural texture when used this way. Use yellow, green, and orange sparingly as these colors have an almost-but-not-quite imitative look that cannot compete with the fresh flower. The work has more charm when it is not imitative. Red is used sparingly, sometimes as an undercoat, and with a little investigation you will develop your own approaches. Silver is a time-saving first coat for designs of flat white, especially for branches, cones, and woody pods. Do not use paint spray on anything to be covered with tape as it will prevent proper bonding.

Fluorescent paint spray, made by Derusto (called Derusto fluorescent), is the only hardware store paint used here. It is available also at florists' supply stores. Its luminous night-glowing quality is very effective in this decorating sphere and especially attractive when slightly overdusted with a bright gold floral spray paint or with glitter dust.

4.   *GLITTER DUST, GLITTER GLUE*

To apply glitter dust, spray the area to be dusted with glitter glue and simultaneously sprinkle the glitter dust. As glitter glue dries instantly, this should be a well-organized process with the glitter dust in a small container like a coffee measurer so it can be applied while glue spray is still wet. When using glitter dust on white or pastel surfaces it is better to use a solution of one-half Elmer's Glue-All and one-half water, and paint on the area with a small brush. Glitter glue has a tendency to turn creamy yellow, while Elmer's Glue-All stays transparent or white.

Quickee hand cleaner is an invaluable asset as it will remove paint from your hands, leaving the skin clean and nail polish intact.

Save excess glitter dust by shaking glitter over box so that it can be used again. Don't throw away the tissues used for masking and for spray boxes as they make lovely art forms or gift wraps.

3 Stemming

1. STEMS

WIRE

If you follow these instructions for stemming step by step the results will be rewarding. You will have a durable form which can be admired and handled without rebalancing or fussing. After you have made your first flower you will be inspired to improve on it and do others.

The purpose of wiring is to articulate the decorative forms and make them adjustable. The structure and balance of the design depend on the correct choice and use of wire. It should be handled so that it is as inconspicuous as possible.

Several weights of wire are suggested as a beginning inventory for these designs. (See page 3.) Not all weights are available in flocked or bound finish. The lighter weights can be bought in stick or spool form. The stick form, though less economical, is easier to use as there are no curves to combat. *Handle spool wire with caution.* It should be tightly re-coiled and fastened into its staple or slot after each use because it can whip dangerously.

There is a wide range of alternate weights of wire. The lower numbers indicate heavier wires. Where light wires are recommended, two or three numbers in either direction might be substituted. For example, for no. 30 wire, 28 or 32 might do. From no. 24 wire to no. 9, which is the equivalent of a wire clothes hanger, malleability decreases markedly. Bound wire is used where no taping is needed to conceal mechanics or where it is fairly dominated by additional material as in the Candle Set (page 105), and Pomander Bells (page 66).

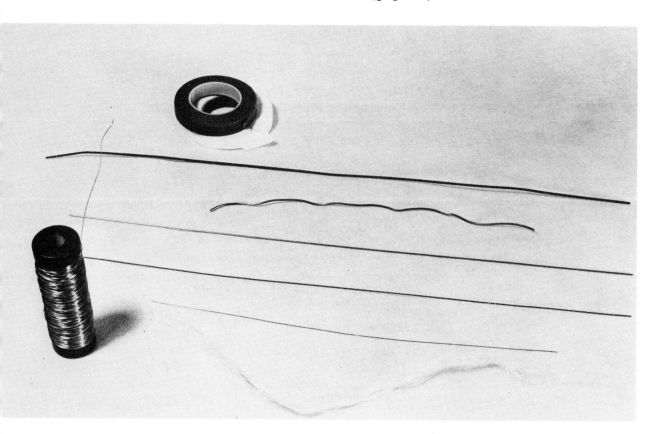

The age and degree of dehydration of materials may vary the recommended stem wire two to four numbers. A flower form composed of fresh sea grape leaves needs a no. 9 stem. A dried leaf form should be supported by a lighter no. 12 wire stem. The length of the stem also changes the wire weight requirement. A flower form of a few well-dried oak leaf petals used in a short-stem set could be constructed on two or three no. 18 wires, whereas a 30-inch-tall flower of many oak leaf petals needs a no. 9 or 10 stem wire. As your enthusiasm grows so will your inventory.

A good main stem supports the weight of the blossoms without weaving or bending when held near the end of the stem. This is of importance particularly if you use a flower in a pinholder for an arrangement. The same standard is used for selecting the wire for the leaf stem. A doubled light wire is often easier to conceal than a single heavier wire. The wire for the flower form, or the throating wire, should be fine enough not to injure the cone or pod, but strong enough to hold it firmly on the stem. Additional wires can easily be added from joint to joint or from leaf stem to end of stem before final taping. In a set design of more than one flower, additional wires are added from joint to joint, but these should be incorporated at the beginning of the assembly or it will be difficult to conceal the mechanics. If materials are substituted, check design balance at each stage before final taping. Keep wire as free of twists and kinks as possible. Bend but do not crease. Curve but do not crimp.

To straighten a sharp bend, ease the wire at both sides of the bend into a parallel position which will open the angle of the bend from a V to a U. Keep bending in all directions until the U is free from crimp. The ends or sides can then be spread straight one at a time.

Resist the temptation to simulate wrought iron work with wire and tape. They are only the means to exhibit the design.

These flower forms are made to stand free with all parts showing. This necessitates graceful throating with no evidence of mechanics. Experience in corsage craft may have familiarized you with stemming methods, but this finishing procedure differs because of the need for animation. Firmly coiled calyxes, where the wires are snugged tightly, and parallel supporting wires that align with the stem but do not twist around it, are essential here.

To add a stem to any form is an adventure. A stone of interesting shape, tightly wired inside a fragment of a sheer stocking, neatly throated, sturdily stemmed, and embellished with one or two coarse-textured leaves, can become a special event.

TAPES

Floratape

Floratape is a self-adhesive stretch tape made to be pulled and stretched. It can be stretched to cover twice its length by bias wrapping.

Brown is the color most often used. Moss green, twig, and white are used occasionally. For an evergreen natural color design as in the Three Flower Ivy Branch on page 77, green tape would be a good alternate finish for the twine wrapping used in the picture and takes less time. For an all-white design, tape the stem with white. In a design to be used on a white tablecloth, the flowers show up more effectively while the white-taped stems disappear into the background.

Floratape adheres in proportion to the tension exerted. Firm taping increases the strength of the stem and is essential where more than one thickness of wire is used—throat and other joining points, for example. If it breaks occasionally as you stretch it, that is a good sign as it shows you are using it to full advantage. Start another length of tape by pressing a new piece firmly over the break and it will adhere and blend invisibly. Use the tape in lengths of 10 inches or less until you become used to it. Then you may decide to use the whole roll as you work, but that complicates things until you are adept at the stemming procedure. Do not tape *over* tape except at joints where there would be a natural thickening. It is easy to tear the tape from the roll. For practice, pinch a six-inch length of tape from the roll by grasping between the thumbs and forefingers of both hands and pulling apart with a quick snapping motion.

Take a stick about one-eighth of an inch thick and four to six inches long. Wad a half-inch of the end of the tape into a pebble about one-eighth of an inch thick. Press this pebble end onto the top of the stick. Hold the wad firmly against the end of the stick and wind the tape around the stick and back over the wad to start the wrapping process. Keep pressing tightly with one hand, holding the starting end of tape in place and, wrapping with the other hand, pull and press and wrap, and pull and press and overlap the tape onto itself as you

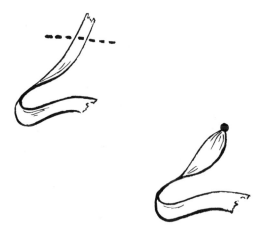

wind around and down the stick on a *slant or bias* toward the end of the stick. This bias treatment prevents a stem from looking bandaged and results in a smooth finish. After about five complete turns around the stem, move the anchor hand from the starting point and place it closer to the wrapping hand. This assures a more even tension and you can then twirl it to complete.

Now try it with a piece of no. 20 wire instead of the stick, being sure to start with the wad. Hold firmly at the starting point, otherwise the tape will slide on the wire as you wrap.

An alternate method of wrapping wire is to tear a piece of tape about two-thirds the length of the wire to be covered. Start with the center of the tape pinched tightly onto the center of the wire, and wrap down to one end. Then, still holding the center spot firmly, turn wire and, using balance of tape, cover remaining part of wire.

Floral Adhesive Tape

Floral adhesive tape does not stretch and is not used for wrapping. It is used when leaves are stemmed with a spine of wire to make them easy to position. This is done only when it is planned to spray the design as this mechanic must be camouflaged unless position is firmly set to conceal the back of the leaf.

Throat the flower you are about to stem and attach a double stem of a single no. 20 wire. If much additional bulk is needed at calyx to make a graceful transition from flower to stem, a small piece of floral adhesive tape (not Floratape) wound tightly around calyx over first throating wire twist will build up the bulk reliably. Start Floratape over the adhesive and continue stemming. Wrap calyx again to thicken it and fit firmly into top of hollow stem. Tape only far enough to hold the blossom securely on the wire stem, which should be long enough to pull through hollow stem. The wire should be very straight so that it goes down through stem without buckling.

This is a good stem to use in an arrangement in water with bold green leaves.

The floral adhesive is also used to hold a bulky leaf joint in place. It is then covered with Floratape.

Coban Elastic

Coban Elastic Bandage, a cloth self-adhesive tape with great tensile strength, is used as a bias wrapping. The narrowest width available is 3 inches. It is an excellent mechanic where additional strength, bulk, or concealment is needed and particularly valuable in clumsy throating and leaf stem joints. When used for stemming it is covered with Floratape. (See page 48, **Arborvitae Wallflower.**)

Both of these adhesives are competent assists for flower arranging when fitting a wired leaf or flower form into a natural hollow stem. Coban holds the wire firmly at stem and throat. Floral adhesive is serviceable wrapped a few times around the bottom of a wire stem to build bulk for placing in a pinholder. It protects the wire from rusting as it is reasonably waterproof.

Hollow stems like plume poppy, sweet cicely, and Indian cup lend drama to arrangements and are easier to set in pinholders than wire stems. Short hollow stems that will fit over the end of wire stems are an assist when Forever Flowers are to be used this way as they not only have more stability in the pinholder but the natural stem protects the wire from water. (See pages 112, 113, 118.)

TWINE

String or twine wrapping gives a stem a handsome texture, whether the flower is delicate or large. A smooth string or a fibrous twine can be very effective on either. In the case of the ivy set mentioned above, the design of the flower seemed to make leaf form unnecessary. A textured stem, since so much stem is apparent, gives the design distinction that waxed tape could not.

String or twine should be unraveled and the single strands applied with a solution of one-half water and one-half Elmer's Glue-All dabbed on every other inch. It is best applied on top of taped or covered wire. Flatten the strand and spread as much as possible. Leave slight spaces so there is no overlap. Start the string a quarter-inch below the area to be wrapped and wrap back up to the area to be covered and back down again to make the beginning firm and smooth. This wrapping should be done on the bias. Finish at the end by sliding the end of the string up under the wrapping for one-half inch with a heavy needle or pin. If the string has to be joined, start again in the same way going back up and over the beginning point to conceal it. When the stem is completed, dip your fingers in the diluted solution and dab around joints and places that seem fuzzy, and let dry. Twine will need this last finishing touch more than string and may have to be clipped a little after it has dried. Spray lightly with antique gold.

BROWN PAPER

Brown paper cut in ½ inch strips is one way to finish a stem. Use on a stem without a leaf form. Pie tape (preglued thin brown paper used to seal edges of pies) already cut is useful instead of cutting paper in strips, and is thin and easy to handle. Dampen the paper lightly so that it stretches. Package sealing tape already glued is likely to be too heavy unless it is very narrow and very wet.

2. ASSEMBLY METHODS

CONES

Garden clippers will cut most of the cones described in this book except for the large western and southern pine cones for which an electric saw is needed.

For most purposes the scotch pine cone is ideal as a base for flowers as it is sturdy and easy to handle and does not require a separate beginning wire around the throat. It can be started and stemmed with no. 26 wire. Large cones are large enough for all but very large flowers; a small cone is good for the lightweight petals or small flowers, and the splits of this cone offer good variety if the stem half is used for an open flower and the blossom or tip end for a full bloom or a bud.

Tip end split

The hemlock cone has many tuck-in places for its size and is fairly sturdy when you get accustomed to handling it. It is used here as a base for the honesty flower and akebia flower. Other lightweight petals will adapt well to it. It can be started with the light no. 30 wire and then joined to the no. 26 wire stem for a neat operation. It is the daintiest of the cones.

The southern and western pine cones are very effective used either whole or split for the large dramatic happy flowers.

For making leaves of the individual cone petals, the Norway spruce cone and white pine cone are excellent. For larger petals, use the southern and western cones. These same cones afford good petal forms for pasting.

Stem end split

White pine cones are very sticky. The sap can be dried out by baking on a piece of aluminum foil, which can be discarded, in an oven set at 200 degrees for one half-hour to an hour. This process spreads the sap and it sometimes brightens or lightens the color of the cones. It also makes the large cones easier to cut, even though more fragile.

A fresh Norway spruce cone or white pine cone can be twisted at the middle to make a start for peeling off petals. Using a small knife pinch the cone petal between your thumb and the knife as you would pare a fruit skin and pull downward along the center core of the cone until the petal comes free.

Cut the small pointed bump off the end of the petal where it was attached to the cone so the work will be smooth.

Quickee hand cleaner will remove sap as well as paint without drying your skin.

Large cone tip split

The flower will be a flat form if stem end is used for the center of blossom, as in the leucothoe, or a many-petaled blossom if the tip end is used, as in the honesty flower and oak leaf flower. The flower can be a great one with a large cone, a medium one with a large scotch pine, and a dainty one with a whole hemlock cone. A cold cone will be narrow and tightly closed but will expand when brought indoors.

Stem end split

Moisture increases malleability. Materials that have been glycerin-treated are malleable. In fact, most materials that have dried naturally are malleable if dampened. Do not soak until you have tried a slight amount of moisture. Fingers dipped in water will often do the necessary work. The dampened object should be clamped or weighted, wired, or roped to dry in the position desired. Do not work with damp material. Tape will not adhere; paste will take a long time to dry, and spray will not stick.

A dampened cone will often close tight and open as it dries.

PODS

Tightly closed pods will often open and stay open if dampened and heated gently. This is a useful technique if you prefer the open flag or iris pod to the closed spike form. In case of heavy pods completely closed, dampen first and help the opening process by slitting the tip with a sharp knife or razor blade along the natural seams at the tip of the pod. Large cone petals, if dampened, can be slit at stem end to insert a hairpin wire stem. A pod can usually be pierced through on either side of the stem. A few minutes' soaking will soften, or a hot needle may make things easier. Some pods will need a small drill. Only experience can guide you in this.

Iris or flag pods, which are useful forms for wiring, can be *pierced through the calyx from side to side* just above the stem. The wires can be covered easily by taping onto the lower part of the pod, keeping the wire taut and winding down the stem to cover a natural-looking, thickened calyx.

Iris or flag and other pods can also be wired by pushing one wire straight up from bottom of stem end through and protruding from the tip. *An embroidery knot* or coiled wire knot is made at one end of the wire. Push straight wire through a single hole made as close to stem at stem end of pod as possible. Coil wire end protruding through and past pod two or three times and carefully pull back down through hole until coil is firmly clinched within pod. The knot can be further secured by adding a sizable glue-soaked wad of cotton to be pulled back into the throat of the pod by the embroidery knot.

If heavy wire is used, a *half oval of bent wire that hooks* back down into the throat will often work as well as the embroidery knot. When all else fails there is always the drill. Two holes give more stability than one.

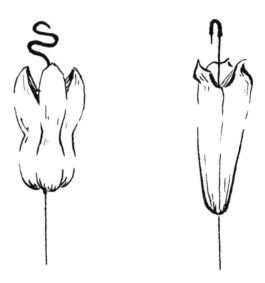

LEAVES AND FLOWER PETALS

For the *double loop wire brace method* tape each of two three-inch no. 30 leaf stem wires for two inches at one end of each wire. Shape the taped end of each wire into a narrow hairpin loop about seven-eighths of an inch long and one-quarter inch wide. Cut small thickened stem edge one-eighth of an inch from end of natural leaf stem to create a uniform stem thickness. Sandwich leaf between two of these taped loops, positioning loops with closed U end at about three-eighths of an inch above leaf stem joint along center spine of leaf both in front and in back of leaf. Pinch the open ends of both loops together and include leaf stem, holding tightly to tape at leaf stem joint, and tape firmly down one and one-half inches of stem. Press loops to leaf to conform to one shape so they do not stand away from leaf.

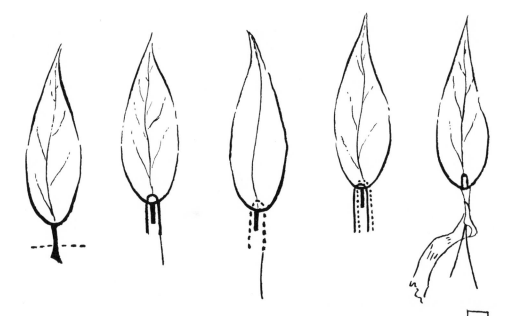

For the *wire spine method* cut strip of floral adhesive one-quarter inch longer than leaf measures from stem end to tip. Place leaf face downward on table. Lay stem wire with end one-quarter inch below leaf tip along center vein of leaf and along leaf stem. Paste adhesive down onto leaf from very tip of leaf to a spot below leaf stem joint. Turn leaf over and bring corners of tape around stem one at a time to wrap over each other slightly, including stem at stem leaf joint. Cut tape away from leaf tip sides shaping to match leaf so it does not

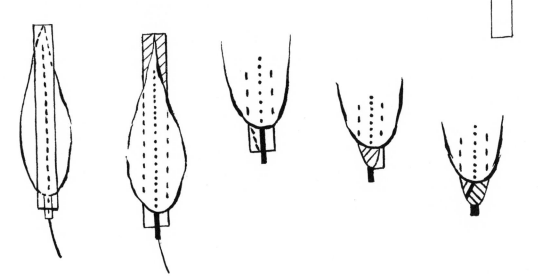

show from right side. If tape does not adhere well, remove it and roughen back surface of leaf with emery board or fine sandpaper. Replace adhesive. Tape firmly with Floratape, bringing tape slightly over leaf at leaf stem joint, and tape for at least two inches down stem: Spray back of leaf with antique gold.

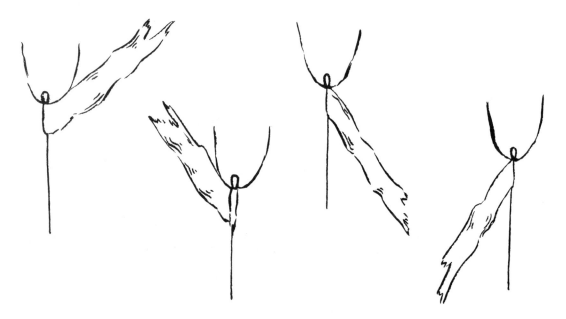

THROATING

The wiring of cone and stem depends on the weight of the cone and the weight of the material used for flower petal and leaf form. Hemlock and small scotch pine cones are the best subjects for this single wiring. One weight of wire is used for throat and stem and for one or more reinforcing wires. (See Honesty Candle Spiral Set, page 92.) The multi-petaled flower formed in M loop bracts without a base also allows use of a continuous wire of any size for any size flower. (See Raspberry Ripple, page 72.) The recurved flower form can be stemmed on a *continuous wire* if it is a lightweight flower or pod shape. The cone base is stemmed in profile. (See page 52.) Otherwise it needs a *prejoined light and heavy wire.* This joins the throating wire to the main stem before the throating wire is applied to the flower form. *A light wire joined to a heavy wire* is the method that can be most generally applied for all kinds of throating. It is ideal with all methods to continue throating wires to a joint, or to end of a stem.

BASE OF SET

The simple *set-base principle* affords versatility in exhibiting climax material. When a composition is assembled to balance on a horizontal surface there are two basic positions.

The *Single Coil* is the elementary balancing position as illustrated in the Oak Happy Flower, page 40. It can be used in a wide C or a circle. Any form can be balanced on a coiled stem base if the weight of the form is centered over the base. The coil can also be used at both ends of or at intervals in a set, either by designing the set to allow for a joint-free stem in area of coil or by adding taped heavy wires, one end joined to the main stem and one end extended for support. It can be shaped in tendrils if other tendril placements are incorporated in the set or finished with a stem-end form of the material used in the design. This is best done for a mantel placement.

In a branched arrangement branches can be extended from the design to coil slightly on the table for balance. Turn the tips upward in a growing attitude.

Any balancing placements should repeat the line of the design so the balancing positions do not detract.

The *S curve* base is used for the horizontal placement of multiple form designs. (See pages 100, 101, Honesty Candle Spiral, page 92.) The assembly can be based by positioning the main stem in one or more areas in an S curve. There are times when both the coil and the

S curve are useful for a single design. (Smilax and Polygonum, page 81.) The set-base principle applies to single or multiple assemblies. Use it to shape the tiny Holidaisy Boutonniere as a table set. It will function equally well when you decide to create a room divider.

Simple Branching Assembly

CHRISTMAS WREATH BOUTONNIERE

1 large Norway spruce cone to yield 18 to 24 pairs of petals, uniform
    size. About 50 petals to allow for mishaps.
brown Floratape
no. 30 wire
2½" red flocked ribbon to be narrowed to ⅜"
absorbent cotton, bobby pins
Elmer's Glue-All, Clearspray or antique gold spray paint

This can be made by continuous taping of individually stemmed pairs of cone petals. Bend and riffle cone as you would break in a new deck of cards and twist to break. This will enable you to peel petals downward off cone core with ease, paring with knife and thumb. Cut knobs off ends of petals, shaping cut to a center point for a nice throating form.

Make cone petal sandwiches. Fill sandwich with wisp of cotton and wire loop. Cut 19 to 24 three-inch strips of No. 30 wire. Form an oval loop three-eighths of an inch long, leaving uneven ends of wire open at ends of loop. Place loop on concave side of petal (the side closest to core of cone) so top of loop fits inside concave area and both ends of wire extend past pointed, cut end of petal. When pinched together, these two uneven ends will form throat and stem. Add a wisp of cotton and a dab of glue in loop area and fit another petal on top so the underside of top petal rounds into the shape of bottom petal. Pinch wires together at throat now for later taping. Clamp with bobby pins or clips and let dry thoroughly for at least fifteen minutes. Tape a strip of petal sets which will then be curved into a circle thus: place one stem of petal set over another petal set so that top petal end just covers throat of lower petal set. Placing petal sets in a line overlapping each placement in the same fashion, until all stems are joined in one strip. Check taping to be sure all wires are held firmly before shaping. Shape strip gently and twist wire of last stem placement under stem of first placement to finish. Apply Clearspray or antique gold paint gently. Do not load with spray. Let dry.

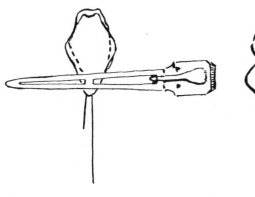

Cut flocked ribbon. if narrow width is not available, to a two and one-half inch length strip three-eighths of an inch wide. Twist twice in center. With a four-inch piece of taped wire, pull twisted area of ribbon tightly between cone petals into spot where circle is joined, twist twice. Conceal ends of wire.

This technique applies to the making of any kind of wreath, adjusting weight of wire to weight of material. For a larger wreath an additional heavy reinforcing wire is essential.

This is effective not only on a dress, suit, or coat but as a circlet for the neck of a gift bottle.

⁴ Single Flowers

1. HOLIDAISY BOUTONNIERE

(Shown in color, Figure 1)

1 acorn cap
2 tulip tree pods (about 20 petals)
1 poppy pod
2 small to medium leucothoe leaves or andromeda leaves (only one
    leaf is used in this picture)
   brown Floratape
1—14″ flower stem length } no. 30 wire
4— 8″ leaf stem lengths }
   spray paint—bright gold, silver
   Elmer's Glue-All, glitter glue, silver dust sparkle,
    absorbent cotton

Pierce two holes three-eighths of an inch apart on either side of stem end of acorn cap. Use a needle or fine nail to make these holes large enough to insert tightly taped No. 30 wire. Tape eight inches of the 14-inch wire. This leaves six inches untaped so successive wrappings of tape will not make a heavy-looking stem as wires are added. Pull untaped end of the 14-inch length of wire up through one

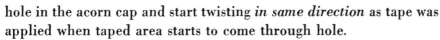

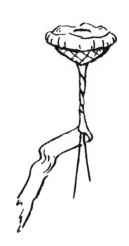

hole in the acorn cap and start twisting *in same direction* as tape was applied when taped area starts to come through hole.

Continue twisting and pulling taped part of wire across and down through other hole in cap until you can pinch a half-inch of taped wire stem with the fully taped wire at throat of cap. Before tightening, fill the area between wire and hollow of acorn cap with a wad of absorbent cotton soaked in Elmer's Glue-All. Tear an eight-inch strip of Floratape; wad one inch at the end of it into a tight pebble and press wadded end tightly against stem end of acorn cap, holding while you twist approximately even lengths of the stem wire tightly twice at the throat joint. Tape throat by continuing tape attached to wad up and over wad and twisted area, at least twice and on a slant, and tape down two inches on what is now a two-wire stem. The first leaf stem will be added at a point one-half inch above where main stem taping was stopped. Tape onto tape at a joint for a firm clinch. Let cotton dry.

Tape one and one half inches of each of the four leaf stemming wires at a point half an inch from one end of each wire. Form hairpin shaped loops one-quarter inch wide with loop center in center of the taped area of each wire. Two wires are used to brace each leaf. Place one taped loop on top of leaf one-quarter inch above leaf stem joint and in line with leaf spine. Place second loop in same way on underside of leaf. Pinch below leaf stem joint to include loops and leucothoe leaf stem from which thickened one-quarter-inch edge has been cut. Tape stem and wires into tight calyx for one inch along stem. Repeat for second leaf. (See page 22, Double Loop Wire Brace.) Add leaves to main stem. Since taping onto tape makes a heavier stem, it is

best done where a joint would naturally thicken slightly. These leaves should extend from the main stem with a stem length of about one inch. Press last taped part of one leaf stem, allowing one inch to remain free, against the last half inch of taped main flower stem approximately two inches below flower. Tape main and leaf stem together for one inch, keeping wires parallel and tape tight and on the bias, overlapping closely as you tape, to give extra strength to joint. Apply second leaf (optional) to opposite side of main stem, about three-quarters of an inch below first leaf, again taping taped leaf stem to taped main stem. Hold all wires tightly with leaf stem wires parallel on top of main stem wires and tape all wires together to end of stem. Coil this stem end around a pencil or small stick for a finishing flourish.

Place tulip tree pod petals in acorn cap to form flower. Dip flat end of matching size tulip tree pods into fair amount of glue and, making opposite placements each time, paste petals on top of cotton packing so the flat ends meet at center of acorn cap. The hook on the outer edge of the tulip tree pod petals should be on the top side of the flower. This is an ideally durable outer edge for the boutonniere purpose.

When petals are placed to form a complete circle, you may choose to add another row on top. If so, select smaller size matching petals and add a good dab of glue on top of center, where previous row of petals meets, before making placements again in opposite fashion and with short petals placed thin edge in center and hooked ends facing up at outer edge. This row should sit easily within outer edge of first row, otherwise flower will look bumpy with overlapped hooks. To complete flower form, dab some more glue in center of flower, slice flat top of poppy pod away from its lower cup, and glue flat top into center of flower.

If flower is to be sprayed, as in picture, spray leaf stem and flower lightly with silver and then with bright gold. This will result in a whitish-gold, bright jewelry look. Dust poppy top and a little more with sparkle by making a window the size of a quarter in a piece of stiff paper or cardboard. Spray glitter glue through the opening so it goes only on area to be dusted and quickly sprinkle silver sparkle onto glue-sprayed area. Let dry two or three minutes. Blow off excess dust. Present this with a corsage pin.

2.   *SINGLE-PETALED HONESTY FLOWER*

(Shown in color, Figure 2)

2 or 3 hemlock cones* (or 1 small scotch pine cone)
7 to 11 large honesty seed petals (white center petals of 3 part
    seed pod)
2   glycerined leucothoe leaves about 3″ long
1—26″ length of no. 26 wire
2—3″ lengths of no. 30 wire and 2—16″ lengths of no. 26 wire
    for leaf stems
    brown Floratape, Elmer's Glue-All, a toothpick

optional: antique gold floral spray paint or brown twine

Wrap Floratape tightly, and on the bias, around the center eight inches of the 26-inch length of no. 26 wire which will be the main stem. Use about seven inches of Floratape. Bend this wire in a U-shaped or hairpin-type loop at center of taped area and push center of hemlock cone firmly into—and against—center point of taped loop.

Tighten loop around center of cone, easing it between petals of cone as you tighten it, and wrap one and one-half times, bringing wires down on opposite sides of stem end of cone. Twist wires tightly once at stem end of cone; pinch together firmly. Align wires parallel by pressing them together until they form a single straight line which will be the main stem. Do not let stem twist. Tape again, starting high under throat or stem end of cone to form a smooth calyx and continue tape (about four inches) to end of previously taped section.

Prepare leucothoe leaves by cutting off a thickened eighth-inch end of leaf stem, leaving about three-eighths of an inch or more natural stem on the leaf.

The double loop wire brace method of leaf stemming, page 22, is used here as this design is not to be sprayed and this system of mechanics makes a neat finish with no concealment necessary.

Tape center inch of the two three-inch leaf stem wires. Tape center inch of the two 16-inch leaf stem wires. Each leucothoe leaf is now

---

*Only one hemlock cone is needed for this flower center, but one or two may fracture at your first attempt. The flower form with this cone center has a delicate air that rewards you for the little extra care. Glycerined, unsprayed smilax leaves can be substituted. They are not white like honesty but if glycerined at their early maturity are a translucent gold-beige.

to be sandwiched between a short and a long wire loop. Form hairpin loops with taped area at center of loop of all four stem wires. Press a leucothoe leaf between one short loop and one long loop, positioning center of loops along spine of leaf and lining up leaf stem to lie between the wires. The loops should extend about three-eighths of an inch onto leaf spine at leaf stem joint on both sides of the leaf. Pinching firmly to hold wires in line with leaf stem and spine, tape a neat throat and continue taping for about one inch.

Join leaf stem to main stem, with leaf tip pointing up toward cone, at area where both wires have not yet been taped. Start taping the two stems together an eighth of an inch over the previous tape and continue taping for one and one-half inches toward bottom of stem. Prepare second leucothoe leaf as you did the first and join to main stem on opposite side, starting slightly above end of previous taping. Continue taping to bottom end of stem, taking care to keep all six thicknesses of wire parallel so you have a straight stem with no twists or spirals.

This stem can be sprayed with antique gold if you wish. If so, mask leucothoe leaves with tissue paper before spraying. Another attractive treatment is to cover stem with brown parcel twine, which should be untwisted completely and used spread out very thin. (See instructions on page 18.) Take either of these steps now so as not to damage the honesty petals, which are prettiest in their natural state without spray, and should not be subjected to twirling.

The honesty seed pod is composed of three superimposed petals. The center petal is white and is attached to the stem. This is the one you use for the flower form. If the three petals are still attached they will separate easily if you pinch the point of the petal where it joins the stem and bend it back and forth gently. The two outer covers will fall away with the seeds, exposing the white center petal. Honesty bought from a florist or florist supply shop is already peeled. If, however, you use material from your garden, save the seeds that fall as you peel the pod, and plant them. They stay viable for years and are very easily grown. They are indifferent to soil, sun, or shade conditions. The white blossom opens in early spring with forget-me-nots. The magenta blossom is not quite as pretty but it is worth having this form in either color. Save the outer seed petals as they are useful for many designs. When they have dried green, you have the material for the spiral design pictured on a candle, Figure 7.

Dab glue between cone petals where you plan to place the honesty. Let dry two minutes. Cut stems from honesty petals, taking care not to cut into the protective frame of the petal. Dab small amount of glue on stem end of petal and make petal placements opposite each other, starting with petals nearest the calyx and finishing with the ones nearest the center of the flower. A prettier flower results if you note the curve of each petal and use it to its advantage. Place honesty petals firmly between cone petal rows so they adhere well. Overlap petals on both edges so they do not have a propeller look. A bud type flower is made by turning petals in toward center and placing at center of cone. A more open flower results from placement near cone calyx.

You may have to pry the tiny cone scales apart to insert the honesty petals. Do not try to force the honesty as the glue softens it immediately and it will break or crumble. Use a toothpick or small stick as a wedge to hold cone petals apart long enough to insert the honesty firmly. The finished flower form will show the prong on the outer edge of each petal as in the picture.

3. *HONESTY ROSETTE FLOWER*

(Shown in color, Figure 3)

1   small scotch pine cone
2—30″ lengths of no. 26 wire
4—20″ lengths of no. 26 wire
2   glycerined viburnum or leucothoe leaves about 3″ long
     about 30 white honesty seed petals
1   wild cucumber seed pod (optional)
     about 16″ of hemp or manila twine
     brown Floratape, Elmer's Glue-All, 3 small clothespins,
     1 Coca-Cola bottle, antique gold floral spray paint

Tape center 10 inches of both 30″ lengths of no. 26 wire. Form each into a hairpin-shaped loop with top of loop centered in taped

area. Push pine cone inside loop of wire at center of taped area as near the row of cone scales at the stem end of the cone as possible. Pull loop tightly one and one-half times around cone, wedging it between bottom petal rows, and extend ends of wire on opposite sides of cone.

Repeat this process with second wire, placing the taped loop center of this wire between the row of cone petals just above the first loop and again bring wires down on opposite sides of cone. All four wires should extend from cone at slightly different places. Tighten these wires and twist once *between* the twist of the first wire and the bottom of the cone. This will ensure a firm placement of the flower head. Arrange all four wires so they are parallel and, pinching firmly, tape high under cone base for a smooth calyx and continue taping stem made of four thicknesses to where leaf stem will be joined—about five inches.

The rope wrapping of the stem begins here. (See twine instructions, page 18.) Unravel the skeins of the string and dampen slightly to control hair ends more neatly. Start wrapping just below calyx with a good application of full strength glue, wrap up and over first placement to conceal end of string and continue downward trying not to overlap (not difficult if you keep string on a bias or slant as you do the tape) to the point where first leaf stem is to be joined. Clamp clothespin over calyx until starting point is dry. Make a small neat coil of balance of string and clamp to main stem just above joining area to get it out of the way while you add first leaf.

Stem each of the two leaves according to double loop wire brace method (page 22) and tape leaf stem for one and one-quarter inches. The leucothoe leaf is more durable and easier to handle than the viburnum but they are both effective with this flower.

Rope each leaf stem for about one and one-quarter inches with a separate strand of manila twine just as you did the main stem. Cut rope neatly at the finish and clamp at the end of the roping area on one leaf stem. Apply the other roped leaf stem at area on main stem just above where tape stopped on main stem and tape for about one inch. Unclamp main stem and, keeping it taut, continue roping down main stem to cover newly taped area. Again clamp balance of main stem rope in coil above first leaf. Unclamp second roped leaf stem and apply to main stem on opposite side of first leaf placement. Start joining tape just above previous taping and tape all wires tightly together (taking care not to twist) to bottom of stem, which is now made of six thicknesses of wire. Unclamp main stem rope and, adding diluted glue with every other twist, continue roping balance of main stem.

Mask cone with tissue paper to leave natural brown. Spray stem and leaves lightly with antique gold to blend string and leaf. Be sure to spray undersides as well and let dry thoroughly. A Coca-Cola bottle is just about the right height to anchor the stem while you place the honesty flower petals. They cannot all be done at once or you will unsettle the first placements with the next ones, so a holder is handy.

Dribble glue into crevices around cone between two bottom rows of cone petals. For this design make two placements all around in the row nearest the calyx. Make opposite placements each time to avoid spiral effect. Let glue dry for a minute or so while preparing the honesty seed petals. (The instructions are given in the design of the Single-Petaled Honesty Flower, page 33.) Dot each petal stem end with glue before placing. Begin placement at bottom row of cone, working all the way around with these petals curving downward so they cup slightly around the calyx. Now begin placing all the petals with an upcurved expression, making another row right on top of the first so you are gluing petal on petal. Use glue only at stem end of petals so as not to spoil the airy translucent effect. Let dry after first two rows for a few minutes and proceed again with opposite placements each time to insure an even balance. The rest of the flower petals can be placed with just one row between each row of cone petals.

If you would like to try the seed pod of the wild cucumber vine pasted over the center of the cone instead of leaving the small petals of the cone for the flower center, cut off the three top cone petals. Use a sharp firm clipping approach so as not to jiggle the newborn flower. Paste cucumber pod with a generous application of glue into the flattened cone center. The seeds in the cucumber pod often do not shake out when you begin your work and it is interesting to see your made-up flower disgorge a seed or two long after it was created. The seeds are a lovely form for flower centers or pasting. Do save them. The outer leaves of the honesty seed pods are also excellent flower petals and should be saved as well as the seeds.

4. *OAK HAPPY FLOWER*

(Shown in color, Figure 6)

1   tip or blossom end of a large pine cone about 3″ in diameter and
      3″ long
     about 60 leaves of small and large untreated white oak or pin oak
      (white oak in picture)
2   well-dried lengthwise strips of banana skin
1—30″ to 40″ length of bailing twine, or manila or hemp string
2—20″ lengths of no. 26 wire for cone throating
1— 7″ length, 1—10″ length, 1—26″ length and 1—30″ length of no. 26
      wire for leaf stems
1—30″ length of no. 10 bound wire
     Coban bandage, a sharp paring knife, brown Floratape, Elmer's
      Glue-All, 2 large snap-type clothespins
     floral spray paint: gold, bright and antique, bright red, silver,
      and delphinium blue
     light wire joined to heavy wire

This design has two equally appealing phases. It can be made of mature green oak leaves that have just begun to color and will keep their natural hues for a few weeks. The design can then be sprayed bronze, gold and silver, or multicolor. The pictured flower has a paisley effect due to the leaves being sprayed with many colors before the flower was composed. The last step is slightly more trouble but is worth it. (If you care to make it as pictured, refer to the spray paint instructions on page 9.)

If, luckily, the cone you select has a hollow core, it will facilitate the cone and stem joint. Usually it does not. Be sure the bottom end where the cone was cut is neat so that the petals will form a symmetrical calyx. Peel off extra petals until you achieve this effect. A hot nail or strong sharp knife may make a slight indentation in the center of the stem end or cut end of cone core which will enable you to get an easy joining clinch with no. 10 main stem wire. If not, a pad or wad of Floratape will do the work as it did in this flower.

Tape center eight inches of each 20-inch length of no. 26 wire. Use this center taped area to wedge around cone core just above bottom row of cone petals at cut end of cone. Pull tight and wind around cone core one and one-half times in between the two lowest rows of cone petals, bringing wires out on opposite sides of cone, and pull down to bottom of cone. Twist once firmly and wedge a half-inch round wad of Floratape against cut end of cone inside the bottom wire twist. Use second 20-inch length of no. 26 wire to draw through row of cone petals above the one just wired. Start the center part of the taped area just above, where one of the previous wires extends from the cone so that the one and one-half twist will result in opposite wire placements that alternate and thus form a neat calyx.

Peel away the binding of the 30-inch length of no. 10 bound wire for seven inches at one end. A sharp knife is essential. This unbound end will press against the bottom of cone. Wedge this main stem wire against wad of tape and/or hole in bottom of cone, twist the last cone throating wire once around main stem and first throating wire, keeping main stem very tightly pressed against cone bottom, and wrap one end around under first twist and back under last twist, keeping the winding wires close to each other so the area where stems are joined by twisted wire is no more than three-quarters of an inch long. Now align all four wire ends parallel with stem and pull down straight and tight against the stem.

Start at base of cone throat to wrap cloth adhesive tape on the bias to firm the calyx and smooth over the area of twisted wires. Continue adhesive on the bias down main stem, keeping all wires straight and parallel, to seven inches below calyx where the first leaf will be added. Cover this adhesive taped section with firm bias wrapping of Floratape.

Cut heavy stem ends from banana skins after moistening slightly at area to be cut so they do not fracture. Shape the cut ends, which will be the stem ends, so they graduate gently into leaf frame with a blunt stem end no wider than three-quarters of an inch. Let dry. Spray thoroughly with two light applications of antique gold and again let dry.

Prepare rope or hemp (bailing twine is used in the picture but is not generally available) as on page 18. Separate skeins by unraveling to thin flat strands of about eight threads. This stem covering is used for texture, not strength, and is most effective when sparsely applied. It should overlap only at beginning, joining, and end areas.

Prepare diluted solution of Elmer's Glue-All and water. Dab onto stem as you wrap the string about every inch and rub around in direction of wrapping to keep string smooth and taut. Start with thinly spread strands one-half inch below the calyx. Secure to main stem with one inch of cloth adhesive and wrap back up and over starting point to high under calyx. Apply full strength glue and wrap back down taut and on a slant, dabbing and rubbing, to seven inches below calyx where leaf will be joined. Clamp clothespins over calyx and at end of roping to keep taut while drying. Coil unused string neatly and fasten lightly to roped area with a piece of fine wire to keep out of way during next step. Prepare stems for banana leaves, as described in the double loop wire brace method on page 22.

Tape center five inches of seven-inch length no. 26 wire with Flora-tape. Tape center six inches of 10-inch length of no. 26 wire. Tape end six inches of the 26-inch and 30-inch lengths of no. 26 wire. The banana skin leaves will each be pressed between a short and a long wire. Place one banana skin between the 10-inch and 30-inch lengths of wire which are bent into a loop at the center of their taped area. The outside of the skin is best used as the outside or side away from the main stem. The taped loop should extend a little farther along the outside of the leaf—about three inches from the stem end—than the inside loop, which should extend past the stem end at top side of skin for two inches. With Coban, tape bottom two inches of banana skin firmly braced within these two taped loops to end of leaf stem and tape to main stem over same area. This shows no stem on the leaf but has the effect of a sessile or clasping leaf.

Unfasten excess string, dab it with diluted glue, keep it taut, and continue roping to the end of this new joint. Align long untaped wire parallel with stem to keep out of way and again tie coil of unused string on upper stem to prepare for next leaf joint. Make a loop at center of taped areas of both remaining wires. Sandwich second banana skin securely between the two loops, with the shorter loop on inside of skin to face the stem and the longer one on the outside. Place the longer loop onto the leaf slightly farther from the stem end than the shorter loop as in first leaf placement. Tape skins securely within loop braces, tape again to main stem, fastening entire taped area, and continue downward to bottom of stem, keeping both long extra wires in line with stem as you secure them with Flora-tape. Do not let them twist.

Untie the unused string and, dipping and rubbing with diluted glue solution, continue wrapping to end of stem. Finish neatly by tucking the end up under the wrapping for at least three-quarters of an inch. Let dry. Remove clothespin at throat and clamp onto stem end. Spray stem, leaves and cone with antique gold. Let dry. Remove clothespins. Press loops and banana skins to conform to one shape to minimize the wire effect and gently adjust position so tip of leaf is pointed upward.

Put oak leaves in a large spray box, spread apart in random fashion and follow instructions on spray paint, given on page 9. Only the upper half of the leaf will be seen and the stem will be cut so do not bother with stem ends. Use blue first, red second, silver third. Let dry. Shake and repeat. Fork the leaves over so the spray now coats the other side of the leaves. Spray in the same way, let dry, shake, and repeat. Let dry.

Dribble glue around bottom row of cone petals. Cut stems and ends of leaf from oak leaves to where leaf end is at least three-quarters of an inch wide so it will glue firmly. Dab each leaf with glue as you place it and make opposite placements each time. Place small oak leaves all around and deeply into cone, touching the core, between the bottom two rows of cone petals. Dribble glue into core of this row again and let set a minute. Place a second row of larger leaves right side facing the tip of the cone and glue them on top of first row, gluing at core area only. Continue gluing large leaves between next row of cone petals in the same fashion until the row next to the tip of the cone is reached. Here is where the flower center is most effective if your final leaf placement is of very small leaves and only the tip of the cone still shows. Spray lightly and quickly with bright gold to highlight the flower.

To position stem as in Figure 6, use lower half to two-thirds of stem for coil. Do not force. Bend lower half of stem into a wide C and let the bound wire guide you in closing the C to a circle of approximately seven inches in diameter. Then move the lower stem as it curves into the C so that it positions the flower over the center of the circle. If you do this a little at a time the wire will co-operate and the tape or string will stay firmly glued.

5. *RAINFLOWER*

1   stem end of large split pine cone, 3 full petal rows on this split
      (the one pictured is a longleaf pine cone)
6 to 9 extra petals of pine cone
      about 60 tip ends of coconut seed fronds (scotch broom is a
      fragile but possible alternate)
2   large glycerined leaves of false spikenard (or false solomon's
      seal) (glycerined rhododendron or magnolia may be
      substituted)
1—30″ length of no. 10 bound wire
2—10″, 2—7″ and 1—12″ lengths of no. 26 wire for leaf stems
2—18″ lengths of no. 26 wire for throating cone
      small box of absorbent cotton balls, Coban bandage, hemp or
      manila twine (about 1 yard), Floratape, 2 clothespins,
      2 bobby pins, Elmer's Glue-All, floral spray paint, silver,
      bright gold, and antique gold

Follow instructions for throating cone in Oak Happy Flower,
page 40, using taped center of the two 18-inch lengths of no. 26 wire
and attach to no. 10 wire, the binding of which has been peeled back
seven inches. Cover throating wires in same fashion as for Oak
Happy Flower, first with cloth adhesive tape, then with Floratape,
and then with fine strands of rope to seven inches below calyx, where
leaf stems are to be added. Clamp beginning and end of twine with
clothespins. Tie excess on upper stem.

Spray spikenard leaves on both sides with silver. Let dry. Form
wire hairpin-shaped loops of both 10-inch lengths of no. 26 wire
by taping center five inches and bending loops at center of taped
area. Tape center four inches of seven-inch wire and center six inches
of 12-inch wire and bend with loop at center of taped area. Spray
taped part of loops on both sides with silver on both sides. Let dry.
Make braces of loops for first leaf, placing shortest loop of seven-inch
wire on top of right side of leaf along leaf spine one and one-half
inches above the stem end of leaf with loop pinched tight along sides
of natural leaf stem. Place second loop made of 10-inch length wire

along back spine of leaf two and one-half inches along underside and pinch stem between two wire ends. Tape leaf loops and stem one inch, including leaf stem joint.

Cover taped part of stem with a few strands of string, pasting and securing as for main stem. A bobby pin, curl set clamp, or paper clip will secure the twine wrapping after gluing at the stem leaf joint. The end of the wrapping can be taped immediately to main stem. Tape leaf stem onto main stem, leaving little more than two inches of leaf stem standing free, and continue taping onto main stem down to end of leaf wires. Uncoil unused twine and unclamp at last wrapping point. Keeping tension on twine, add full strength dab of glue and continue to rope down stem to end of Floratape on this leaf stem. Dab with glue, clamp to secure, and prepare second leaf. Form loops with center of tip in center of taped area of the remaining two 10-inch lengths of sprayed, taped no. 26 wire. Place one 10-inch wire loop on top of leaf spine running along spine three inches above stem leaf joint. Press leaf between this loop and the other loop, which should run along bottom of leaf and along leaf spine for a little more than three inches.

Align wires firmly along spine and stem of leaf and, pinching tightly, tape from one inch above leaf stem joint, clasping leaf stem closely to main stem and continue to tape to main stem with no free stem extending. Unclamp string joint, untie excess, dab with full strength glue and, keeping tension on string, with diluted glue and, rubbing in same direction as wrapping, continue to wrap to bottom of main stem. Finish carefully and clamp with clothespin to dry. Mask leaves with tissue and spray stem with antique gold to blend string and stem. Let dry. Remove tissue and spray stems and leaves very lightly with bright gold. Let dry and place coconut fronds between cone petals.

Use in groups so there are four to eight long points in each group. Do not include any stem that is thicker than one-eighth of an inch. Paste each group together with wisps of cotton. Make all the groups and let dry before pasting into cone. If cone petal rows are wide-spread, pack slightly with cotton wisps, not wads, and dribble glue generously over cotton near cone core before pasting in cone. Place first groups a half inch apart from each other between two bottom rows of cone petals. Let dry at least ten minutes or until firm. Place additional cotton wisps around cone core in between same row of petals with generous amount of glue. After five minutes add alternate placements of frond groups in same cone petal row on top of glue-soaked cotton, adding glue with each group placement. The silhouette should now be a circle, wispy at the outer edge and solid in the center around the cone.

Continue glue and cotton wisp placements in between second row of petals in the same manner. Allow drying time so that new placements don't disturb previous ones. Cut group ends neatly and take care to hide cotton wisps in last placement under center cone petals which are now the top of the rainflower. Let dry for one hour before spraying flower lightly twice from all sides with silver floral spray paint. Let dry.

Turn upside down gently and paste extra cone petals, neatly finished at stem end, onto back of calyx to cover cut ends of petals. Put glue on cone first and let dry a few minutes before applying calyx petals. Turn tips of petals to be added all in same direction. If they fit best with tip curved downward, paste all that way. Keep paste around the calyx area to leave tips on outside free and airy and do not paste onto throating wires. Let dry and spray calyx and back of flower with antique gold. Let dry. From a distance spray leaves and flower form very briefly with bright gold. Stem need not be masked as this is just a highlighting which will not spoil the stem if any spray should settle there.

6. *ARBORVITAE WALLFLOWER*

(Shown in color, Figure 4)

1   stem end split of large pine cone with about 3 full rows of petals
        and about 10 extra petals for finishing calyx
     about 20 branches of fresh arborvitae, 10″ long
2   medium to small palm paddles
2—18″ lengths for throating cone ⎫
2—12″ lengths for leaf stemming ⎬ no. 26 wire
2—26″ lengths for leaf stemming ⎭
1—30″ length no. 10 bound wire
2   yards red and silver aluminum and plastic gift wrap ribbon
        or string
     floral spray paints: silver, bright gold, holiday red or
        fluorescent red
     Floratape, Coban Elastic Bandage, Elmer's Glue-All,
     pre-joined light and heavy wires

Alternate: cedar or juniper keeps well if used outdoors in winter;
        coiled 30″ lengths of wisteria make an easy leaf type placement

Trim cone split so cut end petals are neat. The finishing step will hide them if they are evenly cut.

Attach cone to main stem as in Oak Happy Flower, page 40, or by joined wire method, which may be easier. Proceed by joining both throating wires to main stem as a double extension of main stem. Tape just six inches of one end on both throating wires. Scrape top two inches of end of bound wire which will be the main stem. Extend the main stem by adding a throating wire on both sides of last two inches of scraped main stem. Tape two end-taped inches of one throating wire to last two scraped inches of mainstem with Floratape. The extended wire will be 46 inches long. Tape second throating wire in same way on opposite side of main stem, including previously joined taped section, with Coban bandage cut to one-inch width. Tape these three wires together for three inches, using Coban on bias as with Floratape. Both of these throating wires will now be twisted around cone one at a time and brought down as part of the main stem.

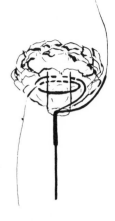

Wad a two-inch strip of Floratape into a tight ball. Impale ball on end of main stem between two throating extensions and press tightly to cut end of cone, which will be the cone throat. Hold Coban-wrapped joint tightly with one hand to relieve the stress on the main stem throating wire joint while you wrap taped part of throating wire at left of main stem around cone core between two bottom rows of cone petals one and one-half times. Bring wire out of cone at opposite point from start, pull down tightly to clinch cut end of cone on main stem, and tape wad. Twist once firmly around main stem as close to cone end as possible. Pull taped part of second throating wire one and one-half times around cone between same row of petals if there is room, otherwise between row of petals above previous throating wire wrap. Take this throating wire across from right to left and twist around cone one and one-half times, coming out of cone and down to cone throat opposite where it went into cone.

Without releasing grip on wire joints, twist second throating wire once between cone bottom and first wire twist and once again below the first wire twist, keeping twists as close together as possible. Align the two long ends of stemming wire down sides of main stem and tape high under throat and firmly for seven or eight inches to where first leaf will be attached. (See string instructions on page 18.) Cut a 26-inch length of metallic ribbon. Cover stem from the throat of the cone to the end of the taping on main stem. Be sure to glue well. Clamp ribbon at throat to dry and clamp at end of wrapping. Tie excess ribbon on upper stem so it is out of the way until ready for finishing.

Stem the palm paddle leaves by making holes with a hammer and nail or soak a few hours to soften so a heavy needle will penetrate. Cut stem of paddles to two inches. Shape into a narrow tapering end. Pierce four holes in each leaf: two holes at base and center of leaf close to stem and one and one-half inches apart, and two holes one inch higher on leaf, one inch apart, so they can be wired across the leaf at a right angle to the stem. Make holes just the right size for wire. If taped wire is used be sure to twist it through the holes in same direction as it was taped so as not to riffle the tape. Tape all four leaf stemming wires for five inches at center of each wire.

Pull the short leaf stemming wire, with center five inches taped, through the holes nearest the stem so ends come out on the hollow or silver side of the paddle and taped loop is on back side of leaf. Put the other long leaf stem wire, with center five inches taped, so it comes through the leaf in reverse. The center taped area will be on the front or hollow side and the long untaped ends will come out on the back or red side of the leaf.

Bring the long wires around and twist in front, including the leaf stem and the two shorter wires, and twist around in back again and pull down sides of leaf stem. Wrap leaf stem throat with Coban for an inch and one-half or just short of end of leaf stem. Be sure to wrap on bias.

Apply glue to throat stem area. Cut a twelve-inch piece of ribbon. Tape leaf end throat almost to end of Coban wrapping. Clamp at beginning and end of ribbon wrap. Do not cut ribbon until ready to finish. Stem second leaf in the same fashion. Use a 40-inch length of ribbon to start the ribbon throating on this second leaf, glue well, clamp at throat and finish point and coil ribbon so it is out of the way when stem is attached to main stem. Wrap Coban around first leaf stem and main stem at a point where ribbon stopped on main stem and on leaf stem and on the bias to include leaf stem wires and main stem for three or four inches. Unclamp ribbon on upper stem where wrapping ended, add glue, pull ribbon tight, and continue wrapping ribbon down past joining points of stems to where next stem is to be added. Wire ribbon to keep tight as clamps would be in the way.

Remove clamp at end of ribbon on leaf stem wrapping and finish with a snug joint as in string instructions. Attach the leaf stem to main stem with Coban wrapping. Tape the rest of the main stem with Floratape, including paralleled stemming wires, to the end of stem. Add glue to leaf stem last joined and untie ribbon. Glue and wrap ribbon down over stem joining and continue to wrap and glue ribbon to end of main steam.

Let glue dry and spray paddle leaves as in picture, masking the ribbon stem, red on outside of leaf, silver on inside.

If using string finish instead of ribbon, spray silver paint on stem and paddles first. Then mask when dry to spray red paint on other side of leaves. Glue cone core between petal rows generously. Let set ten minutes.

Paste six-inch lengths of arborvitae, placing opposite each time, in between bottom rows of cone petals. Add glue next to cone core. Let set while placing opposites of four-inch lengths in between next row of cone petals. Add glue to this last row close to cone core. Go back to first row and pack with random placements but match length of placements with opposites. Repeat in row above. Let dry one hour. Paste extra cone petals on bottom end of cone to form neat calyx.

When dry, spray flower form with bright gold, then with silver. Too solid a coat of silver is harsh. Go back over it lightly with bright gold spray from a distance. (Check instructions on spray paint on page 9.) The cone center will need less spray than the green leaves.

Juniper or cedar, if used outdoors, is a substitute form. Cedar dries too quickly for indoor use. Two coiled vines of wisteria sprayed with red and silver paint before attaching to stem are a handsome substitute for palm paddles. Dampen first and coil tightly overnight before using. Spray when dry and while still in coil. Remove coil wires or ties when dry and spray again.

7. *RUBBER PLANT*

(Shown in color, Figure 5)

This is made the same way as the Oak Happy Flower (page 40), with the stem coiled twice to balance the heavier petal form. Digger pine petals are used for leaf form (page 56). Cotton wisps soaked in glue and an occasional jigger of linoleum paste help to hold the heavy glycerined leaves in place. It is easier to make with smaller rubber plant leaves for the flower form.

5

Flower Sets

TWO-FLOWER SETS

1. LEUCOTHOE

60 glycerine-treated leucothoe leaves (or glycerined leaves of small
     rhododendron, magnolia, large andromeda, or physostegia)
2 medium-sized scotch pine cones
1—24″ length of no. 12 bound wire for main stem
4—16″ lengths of no. 30 wire for throating
16 to 22—5″ lengths of no. 30 wire for leaf stemming
    Elmer's Glue-All, Floratape, Coban bandage 1″ wide
    floral spray paint: gold, antique and bright
    pre-joined light and heavy wires

    Tape center seven inches of all four lengths of no. 30 wire. Tape
the first two inches of the taped section of two of these wires onto the
last two inches of the main stem wire on opposite sides of the main

stem so balance of taped section extends past end of main stem wire. Use cloth adhesive bandage on the bias to cover this two-inch joint.

Holding the joint securely in one hand to counter the pull of the other, pull taped throating wire up around center of cone core, holding cone sideways and poking main stem hard against cone core center. Wind taped throating wire twice around cone and bring down below cone to high on the cone stem joint. Wind around joint once, twist as high on cone stem joint as possible, and bring ends of this throating wire down at either side of main stem, keeping parallel along opposite sides. Do the same thing with the other extended throating wire, holding the original area of taped throating, including the last wire twist, firmly in the one hand while pulling this wire around cone twice and down to twist again as high as possible under cone around cone stem joint opposite first throating twist. Pull ends of this last placed wire down along sides of stem parallel to first two throating wires and in alternate positions so they come down main stem aligned on all four sides. Then repeat this step with the other pine cone on the other end of the main stem. Tape throats for two inches.

Position these two cones on the main stem to balance.

This is the balance principle on which all the set designs are based. Depending on the weight of the flower head (the cone and petals) and the strength of the main stem wire, any number of flowers can be taped together in a set and arranged to balance. After experimenting and achieving the balancing of a two-flower set, the others will be easy to handle.

In order to know where the leaves should be attached to the main stem, the design must be positioned first. Ideally the petals should be inserted in the flower form to give the perfect balance adjustment. It is easier to complete the design, if, knowing that the petals you will use will form a flower five inches in diameter, you create your balance tentatively, since adding leaves to the main stem after you have placed the flower petals would put undue stress on them.

Lay stem on table flat with cones lying on their sides at both ends of stem. Smooth out any curves or kinks. Bend, do not crease, the first seven inches at one end into an upright position. Repeat with the first 10 inches at the other end. Coil the center remaining part of the stem into a circle and then push one stem base slightly within that circle, keeping cones upright. Adjust any sharp bends into curves and if necessary widen the base circle to achieve an easy balance. No part of the stem should rest on any other part. (See the pictures in this chapter, of the Sachet.)

Add leaves prepared as in the methods shown for double loop wire brace, page 22.

Prepare eight to 11 leucothoe leaves of varied sizes to be used as leaves on main stem. Join them so one group of three to five leaves runs along flat base of main stem. Place small leaf nearest flower form and, using Floratape, attach each successive leaf, graduating the sizes so that the largest leaf is placed last. Tape firmly with four or five bias wrappings at each placement so that the tip of each leaf placement overlaps the previous leaf calyx by one inch. Keep leaf stem wires parallel to main stem wire.

Attach the rest of the leaves to main stem with small leaf nearest flower about five inches below flower.

Add flower petals: cut stems off leucothoe leaves for petals. Apply glue to top side of cones at core.

Place matching size petals in opposite placements between pine cone rows starting at calyx row. Complete lowest row and repeat opposite placements for one or two more rows using matched smaller leaves for each row and alternating placements so no leaf exactly overlaps the one in the row beneath.

Adjust balance. Spray lightly with antique gold and again lightly with bright gold.

The two-flower set technique was the answer to an arrangement problem for a breakfast banquet requiring fresh green decorations for 80 tables. Two two-flower sets were made for each table from fresh sea grape leaves treated with clear spray and refrigerated until the eve of the banquet. Long stemmed sea grape flowers with fresh palms were used for the head table design. The flowers went home with the guests and stayed bright and fresh for two days. They turned pale green and then beige, continuing to be decorative through all phases. As this leaf allows for clear spray absorption, they could then have been sprayed with paint for another function.

2. SACHET

4 dried coconut pod calyxes (2 small, 2 medium)
1 cup of dried lavender
4 large flat acorn caps
6 petals large pine cone
1—20″ length no. 14 bound wire for main stem
8— 6″ lengths no. 30 wire for small blossoms and cone petals
6—10″ lengths no. 30 wire for large blossoms
    brown Floratape, Elmer's Glue-All, absorbent cotton,
      heavy needle or small nail
    sharp knife, cone petals, large haircurl clips,
      antique gold spray paint

Alternate: rose geranium filling inside same pod

Prepare cone petals for leaves. Soak stem ends of cone petals for a half-hour in container such as a spray paint can cover, so that only ends are wet. Cut bottom end bump away, shaping end of petal in a point for neat throating. Wedge knife into the softened cut end of petal and pry open a layer of one-half inch of cone petal to insert a hairpin-shaped wire loop which will become the stem. Add a wisp of cotton and a good dab of glue. Clamp with hair curler and set aside to dry.

Pour glue inside hollow bottom and sides of coconut pod calyx. Poke four holes in each acorn cap in a square pattern. Cross the 10-inch wires as you would sew a button, poking ends of wires in hollow side of acorn cap. Pull wire ends down through stem end of coconut caps with ends uneven from two to five inches. Tape first two stems coming from opposite sides of acorn cap onto opposite sides of main stem for one inch. Twist the other ends around main stem twice and align parallel with main stem. Tape from high under throat to joint of cone petal. Pour liberal amount of glue into acorn cap and let set. Add wisps of cotton soaked in glue.

Tape layered cone petal edges back together tightly. If petal is dry and firm when clamp is removed, throat the petal stems with tape from one-quarter inch above cut petal stem down stem end about one-half to two inches, including wire loop. Use picture as a guide for stem

lengths. Tape one placement at a time to main stem and keep stems aligned. Add flower heads at tips of main stem, taping down stems to first leaf joints. Wrap firmly and on the bias. When dry spray generally with antique gold paint. Let dry five minutes. Add more glue to cotton in acorn-coconut base and stuff with lavender leaves attached to stem. To position, see illustration.

3. OAK

about 40 curly oak leaves, any kind of oak (red oak in picture)
2   small scotch pine cones, fully opened (dampen and heat)
2—28" lengths of no. 30 wire
1—20" length of no. 12 bound wire
    floral spray paint: antique gold or gold'n' pearl
    brown Floratape
    Coban bandage
    prejoined light and heavy wire

If picked in late October oak leaves will turn autumnal hues automatically if kept away from light. They are a fine fall holiday accessory in either natural autumn colors or sprayed with gold, silver and bronze, or in multihue with pumpkin floral spray overlaid with bright gold and silver. This flower can be made by spraying the leaves before or after they are placed in the cone. (See instructions for spray paint, page 9.)

Tape six inches at one end of both lengths of no. 30 wire with Floratape. Join first two inches of taped section of each of these throating wires on opposite sides of two inches at end of main stem wire, taping all three wires together for two inches onto end of main stem wire with a firm bias wrapping of cloth adhesive bandage.
Pinch wrapped joined wires with one hand to make sure of joint

and with other hand pull one taped wire around center of cone core between two rows of petals, holding cone sideways on top of main stem with main stem wire pushed solidly against cone core. Wrap cone core twice with light wire, bring light wire down to main stem and twist around main stem as high under cone stem joint as possible without dislodging from joint. Grasping main stem end again to include the first cone wire twist, repeat with second throating wire wrapping around next central row of cone petals. Twist this wire around main stem, below and opposite first throating twist, and then above it close to cone core. Bring balance of both throating wires down parallel to main stem and tape for a few inches down main stem with Floratape. Tape again for an inch every six inches to keep light wires on opposite sides and in line with main stem.

Repeat the procedure, wiring the second cone on other end of main stem heavy wire and, at completion of throating, twist on this end. Guide the second two light wires to align with main stem on alternate sides of stem so all four wires are in line at four sides of stem. Do not twist wire around stem. Pinch again with Floratape at alternate spots along main stem to guide the second set of throating wires parallel and tape entire stem firmly on the bias from cone to cone. Spray stem lightly with antique gold or wrap with hemp or string and spray with antique gold or gold'n' pearl. (See string instructions on page 18, and for position to balance see Two Flower Sachet, page 56.)

Place oak leaf petals in cone. Cut stem from oak leaves and shape stem end to one-half inch or three-quarter inch for good fit into cone. Position cone so tip end is facing upward. Dribble glue generously around cone core starting between two bottom rows of cone petals. Place small leaves in opposite placement right side down around this row. Let dry two minutes. Apply glue at cone core area on leaves just placed and place another row of larger oak leaves, right side of leaves again facing downward. Let dry. Dribble glue between next rows of cone petals, let set. If the space between petals is too wide to hold next oak leaf placement firmly, dot small wisps of cotton near core on lower cone petals to help hold next oak leaf placements. Add glue. Make this row of the largest curliest oak leaves, facing right side up toward tip of cone and placing opposite each time.

A good coat of clear floral spray acts as a preservative and delays the color change but if used, you will not be able to spray again **to** make it bright, because the floral spray paint will not adhere **over** Clearspray.

This makes a good accessory set into a fruit bowl or with a candle.

4. *SPIKENARD*

19 or 20 glycerined leaves of false spikenard or false solomon's-seal
      (varied sizes will increase interest)
2   large scotch pine cones for flower forms
10 small scotch pine cones for stem trim
1—18″ length of no. 14 bound wire for main stem
2—16″ lengths of no. 30 wire ⎱
2—18″ lengths of no. 30 wire ⎰ for flower cones
3— 7″ lengths of no. 30 wire ⎱
2— 5″ lengths of no. 30 wire ⎰ for cones at center of stem
      Elmer's Glue-All, brown Floratape, Coban
      floral spray paints: gold, antique and bright, silver

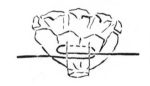

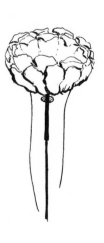

To stem two large cones which will hold spikenard leaves as petals, tape center three inches of each of the 16-inch lengths of no. 30 wires and each of the 18-inch length no. 30 wires. Twist the taped center **of** an 18-inch length no. 30 wire between cone petal rows nearest the bottom of the cone one and one-half times and bring wires down tight, wedging through bottom cone petals, and twist once at cone throat. Twist the taped center of a 16-inch length no. 30 wire around the cone between the next row of cone petals nearest the cone tip and bring down on opposite first wires. Do the same thing with other large cone. Scrape top inch of binding from both ends of heavy 18-inch length of no. 14 bound wire to which two cones will be attached. Wad an inch of Floratape into a small tight ball for packing between main stem end and bottom of cone. Press tip end of scraped heavy wire

against cone with rolled wad at bottom of cone where first wire was twisted and twist the same wires tightly around main stem again. Now twist the throating wire that was placed higher in the cone so these two wire ends are twisted beneath cone and above first wire twist. Twist twice.

Bring all four wires down along main stem, pulling down firmly two at a time and aligning the four wires all around the main stem so that cone is firmly supported. Tape high under throat around twists, with Coban for two inches keeping the tape on the bias and main stem poked firmly against base of cone. Tape over Coban with Floratape and continue taping down stem, keeping the four fine throating wires in line so they do not twist but remain parallel and run along the main stem. Tape until fine wires are concealed.

Repeat this procedure to attach other large cone to other end of main stem wire and tape until the fine throating wires are concealed. This leaves an area in center of main stem where the small pine cones will be attached.

Tape both ends of the two five-inch and three seven-inch no. 30 wires. Twist taped wire ends one and one-half times around the small cones as near as possible to the bottom of the cone and twist twice tightly at the throat. Do this at both ends of these five wires and tape each wire stem from cone throat to cone throat. Tape the center of each of the three seven-inch wires for one and one-half inches at equal three-inch intervals onto the center of main stem and each side of center of main stem. This will conceal the wire at what will be the base of the two-flower set.

Add the remaining two wires on either side of the center wires and tape center two inches of these wires as close as possible to where the last wires were attached. This will make a finishing base for the set. Position the large main cones at tip end of main stem by laying the long assembly flat on the table from left to right. Curve section with small pine cones into an S and bend each stem end on either side upright so cone tips face up. Adjust so it balances well. Spray lightly with antique gold to cover stem and mechanics and cones. When dry, spray cones lightly with bright gold. (See spray paint instructions on page 9.)

Cut stems from spikenard leaves and cut point next to stem so there is a blunt half-inch edge of leaf to clinch to glue within cone petal rows. Place flat in large box and spray lightly twice with silver. Be sure to let dry completely between each application of this silver paint. For highlights, spray once very lightly with antique gold and once with bright gold.

Drip glue around core of cone between rows of petals just above where wire went into cone throat. Use large petals for one flower and small ones for the second flower, or place as in picture with large petals in lower row and small petals above near tip of cone.

Make opposite placements of spikenard leaves in first row and place only three petals on next row which will be the top row. When glue is completely dry, mask stems with tissue and spray bright gold very lightly over leaves placed in cones.

5. *EUONYMUS*

  2   small Scotch pine cones
40   glycerined leaves of euonymus radicans for flowers
  2   glycerined euonymus berry branches with thin stems 4″ long
1–22″ length no. 30 wire for main stem
1– 6″ length no. 30 wire for throating
1–10″ length no. 18 wire for reinforcing
     Floratape, Elmer's Glue-All
     floral spray paint: Christmas red and gold'n' pearl

Tape six inches in center of 22-inch wire and six inches at both ends. Twist center taped section one and one-half times around stem end of cone in between rows of scales nearest the bottom of the cone (page 92). Draw the wires tightly down to center of bottom, or stem end, of cone and twist to form throat. Tape center four inches of six inches of no. 30 wire. Twist this wire around cone one and one-half times between rows of scales above first throating wire, bringing ends of wire out on opposite sides of cone and draw down to a tight twist at center bottom of cone. Twist again for a firm throat. The other cone will be throated with the two ends of the 22-inch wire previously taped. Twist one six inch taped end around second cone and throat as the first cone was throated. Twist second taped end around cone and firm throat in same way as first, being careful to take in slack with this last wiring so doubled stem does not buckle but is firmly paralleled and both wires are the same length. The 10-inch no. 18 wire will now reinforce the double stem wire. Tape one end of this 10-inch wire tightly, high under the throat of one cone for two inches. Add berry stem with tip of stem pointed toward cone just throated, and, leaving tip two inches free, tape, including reinforcing wire, to main stem for two inches. Continue taping toward opposite end of stem and include reinforcing wire for three more inches. Join second berry stem to this three ply main stem and with tips of stem facing untaped cone throat, tape two end inches of this stem to main stem including reinforcing wire. Firm wires together to align and check the length of the reinforcing wire which should fit into last cone throat taping without buckling. Cut excess of reinforcing wire if there is any. Tape throat firmly down to berry stem joint on main stem so no untaped wire is exposed. Form this two flower set into a low form with a coil base by slowly bending three inches on either end of stem upright and gently curving center into a ring. Face cones upright.

Apply glue near cone core in between all rows of cone scales. Cut stems from leaves. Place leaves opposite each time, starting from bottom of cone and working toward top center. When glue is dry, spray the set. (See paint instructions on page 9.) Spray lightly with Christmas red as an undercoat and let dry. Spray lightly with gold 'n' pearl. The result should be a rich cordovan.

BRANCHED SETS

6. POMANDER BELLS

3 or 4—6″ to 8″ long vines of glycerined myrtle, honeysuckle,
   or euonymus
2   kumquats (those pictured are Nagami, which are eggshaped) *
2   well-dried halves of orange, inverted, with outside clean
   and smooth
   box of whole cloves
2 or 3 oz. of powdered alum or orris root
2—12″ lengths no. 30 wire
4— 8″ lengths of green bound wire (or taped no. 26 wire)
   green Floratape if green bound wire is used, otherwise brown
   Floratape
   small piece of string, needle large enough to thread with
   no. 30 wire
   spray paint: silver, bright and antique gold

The vines will need at least a week to absorb glycerin. The kumquats might take longer to dry so that the skin will not tear. Allow
two weeks. These pomanders will stay fragrant for years if made
carefully.

Thread needle with no. 30 wire. Compact wire as much as
possible so as not to make hole in kumquat any larger than necessary.
Insert wire from stem end one-quarter inch to one side of core and
pull half of the wire through to tip end of kumquat. Bend wire very

*The Neiwa kumquat is a smaller rounded form than the one shown in the
picture. It can be used in this pattern but will have to be completely covered with cloves and allowed to hang free below bell, not tightly fitted into
orange, since it would not show. It was used effectively placed firmly into
a gold'n'pearl sprayed orange cap and stemmed in the same fashion as
above, but inverted to be a flower form. It travels around Florida this way
as part of a herb lecture in an arrangement with dried rosemary stalks set
in Styrofoam in a conch shell.

gently to insert again at tip of kumquat a quarter inch away from core at opposite side of core from first wiring. Draw wire back to stem end after padding tip end of kumquat underneath wire with a wad of string to prevent skin tearing. This string will be removed to place cloves in this area after the rest of the cloves have been inserted. Twist wires gently at throat to be used as a handle while inserting cloves. They will be untwisted later.

Insert cloves on an angle toward stem end, starting at tip end with placements so cloves are close but not too close. Peel or scratch off bump ends of cloves before inserting. The remaining end has a more interesting pattern. Start each clove with a fine nail or heavy needle to poke hole first as clove end is blunt and likely to tear skin of kumquat. Place cloves all around tip and two-thirds of the way down to stem end, leaving stem end of kumquat free of cloves in order to fit closely into hollow of orange. Remove wad of string and insert cloves in wire loop area. The orange will be the bell form and the kumquat the clapper form. When all cloves are inserted, shake kumquat gently in alum or orris root inside a small paper bag, coating thoroughly with powder, and hang freely away from sunlight to dry for at least a week. Orris root is more expensive than alum and has an added fragrance. They both dehydrate the fruit and preserve the sachet scent. Keep alum in a bag for further use.

When the kumquat is dry, insert into orange half in which two holes have been poked three-eighths of an inch apart at center of orange half. If orange is too hard to penetrate with needle, dampen slightly to soften. Let it dry before continuing. Spray oranges first with silver, let dry, and then spray with antique gold and then with bright gold. Uncoil wires so that they come straight from either side of kumquat with no twist, and gently poke each wire up through holes in orange bell.

Wad the first inch of a piece of Floratape, press against outside of orange bell between the two wire stems, and include the wad in two twists. Tape up and over wad tightly and back up and over on the bias to assure firm throat. Continue tape for three inches on one bell and one inch on the other. Repeat all procedures so you have two throated pomander bells. Tape one throat at three inches above calyx (see picture showing this is like an inverted stem) to other throat just above calyx and tape together for one inch. Coil both ends of bound wires or extra taped wires for about one and one-half inches around finger or pencil. These look like tendrils of a vine. Attach a vine to each of these wires by taping carefully around the stem and in between the leaves, starting at one and one-half inches from bottom of bound wire and joining wire to vine for about four inches. This leaves both ends of vine and wire free and natural. Tape one of these bound wire and vine stems to one throating wire of orange and another bound and vine to other stem of orange for about two inches where you stopped main stem taping at the calyx of orange. Add next two bound and vine wires, taping all six wires together carefully in and around leaves for four inches. Leave all ends free. Spray lightly with antique gold on *leaf stems only*, allowing natural green of leaves to show through slightly and taking care not to spray kumquats as this would blot out the aroma. Hang by its curled stem ends.

7. AKEBIA

about 30 petals of glycerined akebia—there are 5 petals to a stem
    (see photograph, page 6)
    (substitutes are glycerined euonymus, glycerined small leaf ivy,
    untreated tiny oak leaves)
5 stem ends of sensitive fern fertile frond picked green if possible
    (pictured is the end of the stem or frond that hooks into the root
    of the fern)
1 small scotch pine cone
2—no. 30 wires 11″ long for throating
2—no. 18 wires 12″ long for stems
1—no. 18 wire 15″ long for stem
    floral spray paints: flat white, flat black
    Floratape, a fine strong needle and a thimble, small pliers

These fern stems should be plucked by placing one hand or a sneakered foot on fern root and pulling hard at bottom of frond. It does not harm plant.

Soak fern stems, if not still partly green, to soften, so that needle will go through vascular channel.

Tape center five inches of both no. 30 wires. Wedge center of one taped wire into row of cone petals nearest stem end of cone and work around, pulling tight until wire is wrapped around cone inside petal rows one and one-half times. Pinch cone to lessen stress as you draw wires down to cone stem end on opposite sides of cone. Twist once under cone stem end. Repeat with second wire, drawing this wire around cone through row of petals just above first wire twist. Draw wire ends out on opposite sides of cone and pull down on opposite sides of first wires. Twist once between cone bottom and first wire twist. Draw four wires down straight and parallel and tape cone throat, pinching two wire twists together to insure firm taping. Tape high under throat for three-quarters of an inch and add the 15-inch length of no. 18 wire to the four throating wires, again keeping all wires parallel. Pinch the heavier wire tight at calyx and tape it pushed between the other four wires with two light wires at either side. Tape down to first joint of a fern frond tendril—about four inches.

Drive a needle into cut ends of all five stem ends of the wet fern fronds as far as possible to prepare for inserting heavy no. 18 wire. Pliers will be necessary to withdraw needle. Use one no. 18 wire end to poke as deeply as possible into each cut end of fern after starting with needle. There are two vertical vascular hollows in each stem which should co-operate. Keep turning and twisting wire to get a channel at least one inch deep. Remove wire once channel is established and assemble flower.

Fern stems are placed like heavy tendrils.

Press 15-inch length wire tight against cone throat and tape again down to first joint where fern stem is to be added. Keep this wire from twisting and line up parallel to other four wire ends as you tape. Push end of a 12-inch wire length into a stem end that has a nice attitude for the placement nearest the flower. Tape wired area of stem smoothly onto taped flower stem slightly above point where flower stem taping ends. Tape one inch over this added wire, including one-half inch of tape and one inch of stem. Wire and tape next fern stem for the second tendril placement. Tape this stem joint together with other two heavy wires and make a second smooth joint just below the first joint. Add a third heavy 12-inch wire to thicken the stem. Tape all wires together to within three or four inches of ends of wire. Insert an end of each of these wires into the remaining hollowed tendrils. Tape the wire tendril joint area securely and tape back toward stem joint where all three wires are taped together. Press tape firmly. Position to balance as in picture. Mask cone tip. Spray stems and tendrils flat black. Let dry.

Spray akebia flat white on both sides lightly from a distance. Let dry. Repeat spray until white is satisfactory. Cut stem ends close at stem end of leaf. Glue petals at cone core area only, making opposite placements each time, starting with larger leaves in bottom row of cone and finishing with small ones at top.

Mask stem carefully and spray a final time with flat white. Let dry before touching. Remove masking.

8. RASPBERRY RIPPLE

(Shown in color, Figure 9)

about 30 leaves of gylcerined coltsfoot for flower petals
2   abutilon pods
3   vertical splits of a banana skin thoroughly dried for leaves
2— 5″ lengths of no. 30 wire for abutilon pods
2—12″ lengths of fine bound wire or taped no. 26 wire for final flower throating
no. 22 bound wire
   (12 wires 14″ long for M braces)
   (42 wires 9″ long for double loop braces)
1—22″ length no. 12 bound wire } for main stem
1—22″ length no. 10 bound wire }
1—16″ length no. 10 plain wire or scrape entire length of a bound wire
   sharp knife, scissors, Coban Elastic Bandage, wisps of absorbent cotton
   Floratape, twig or brown, Elmer's Glue-All, glitter glue
   floral spray paints: delphinium blue, turquoise, holiday red, silver, Christmas red, flat black, gold 'n' pearl, flat white
   glitter dust: blue and silver

Moisten banana skins lightly at stem joint to make a neat cut. Remove stem and shape stem end slightly to a blunt point. Let dry before attaching stem or painting.

Scrape binding from ends of both bound wire main stems. Scrape six inches from stem at one end and three inches at the other.

Make two different kinds of braces to support and stem the coltsfoot leaf flower petals. The double loop will hold the upper and inner placements of the flower form and the M loops will hold the larger lower outer placements. At the final throating, part of the M loop will be bent upward to form bracts under lowest petals.

Bound wire is best for this procedure although taped wire does nicely if bound is not available. Cut about 12 bound no. 22 wires in 14-inch lengths. Shape them into an M loop with center loop measuring three inches long and outside ends of loops one and one-half inches and four inches. (Heavens to Betsy, what would we do without Barbara Goodspeed? Please see sketch.) The top two loops will be folded around a leaf to form a brace above leaf stem in back and front of leaf and the center low loop will be a bract. The long end will be taped into the main stem throat joint.

Cut about 36 bound wires nine inches long for the leaves braced with the double loop method. They are used in pairs, front and back of each leaf. Shape them into open end loops one-half inch wide by bending at three inches from end of wire. The bend will be the center of the loop which is placed just above leaf stem joint on both sides of leaf.

Brace tip leaves (small and center leaves) with these loops according to these instructions and tape for one inch at stem throat joint. To stem petals, see double loop wire brace method, page 22.

Fold the M loop in half vertically so that two loops are flat, one on top of the other. The loop at the bottom is in profile. Fit leaf between two loops so it is braced at the leaf stem joint by the loop tips in front and in back of leaf, with tips of top loops one-half inch above leaf stem joint. Pinch together at point of leaf stem joint and tape for one inch to include the four wire thicknesses at center of loops and the leaf stem. Leave longer vertical wire end completely free from tape. This end will be incorporated into final main stem throating and part of it may become a bract or tendril. The wire loop that now faces downward on leaf stem will bend up to become a bract form at flower throat.

Stem the banana skins for leaves by double loop brace method. Form hairpin loops three inches long, one-half inch wide. Loop ends of each of six lengths of remaining nine-inch long no. 22 bound wire. Apply loops back and front of a banana skin with loop reaching onto leaf at cut end of leaf for two and one-half inches back and front. Pinch the banana skin and press and crimp around loop on concave side so it is tightly pleated together (but not closed onto itself) and tape firmly from one-quarter inch below tip of loop to the cut end of skin. Attach one banana skin stem with Coban, cut to one-inch width, at each end of unbound 16-inch length no. 10 wire with leaf tip facing out from each end. Wrap Coban on bias as you do Floratape. It stretches and minimizes bulk. Tape with Floratape again over these joints to cover Coban and tape entire stem down to and including both stem end joints. Put other banana skin leaf into large spray box with this stemmed pair and paint in this way: Shake paint cans constantly, spraying a little at a time from a distance of at least eight inches and let dry between each application.

Spray floral silver on banana twice to coat and preserve. Spray lightly with turquoise, then with black at random, then delphinium blue, lightly each step, and finally gold'n'pearl. Stem will be covered with tape.

Spray abutilon with red and then flat black lightly. When dry, invert and put large heavy glob of Elmer's Glue-All on bottom of pods.

Paint the coltsfoot leaves. Spray them very lightly with silver. Let dry. Spray very lightly with Christmas red or fluorescent red. Be careful of the fluorescent. It is a heavy paint but is effective if used discreetly. Let dry. Repeat with flat white and then with holiday red and then with gold'n'pearl, letting dry between each light spray. When they are dry, turn them over and spray with Christmas red, then turquoise, then delphinium blue very lightly each time and from a distance.

Assemble flower of coltsfoot leaves which now become petals.

Start Floratape around throat of a small tip petal at point just above where taping stopped and add two or three more tip petals and tape into same spot. Wrap tape around this package of stems six or seven times. Poke end of a no. 12 wire that has been unbound for six inches up through this bound petal package. Twist it gently until wire extends sufficiently so that a firm taping of six or seven bias tight wraps, to cover about one and one-quarter inches, can be applied one-quarter inch below the bare wire tip.

Draw fine wire through tender glue-soaked abutilon pod from side to side to extend two inches at either side of bottom half of pod. Apply whiskers of cotton soaked with glue to pod where wires come out from pod and at underside. Bend wires straight down along sides of main stem tip and press into taped area. Press small wrap of tape around wire to help hold it to stem. Do not exert tension as paste will cause it to adhere if let dry. This last step is a precaution to keep it from shattering and to have it reasonably centered. Let dry for ten minutes, draw main stem back down through package, twisting all the time to where taped main stem point clinches against taped center of packaged group of petals.

Add opposite petals to main stem, continuing taping slightly below each previous taping and wrapping on bias with extended throating wires aligned straight down main stem. Place large petals carefully to repeat attitude of upper, smaller flower in picture one at a time. Tape only the free four-inch wire to the main stem for one and one-half inches, leaving bottom of this wire free from stem. Coil first three-quarter inch of a twelve inch length of a fine bound or taped wire and wrap *tightly, horizontally* and *evenly,* around taped area at center of loops of petals just added to main leaf. Do this for an even, tightly aligned coil about one and one-half inches long. Finish wire in another free coil at end to keep the bract loops company. Bend loops and ends of throat wires that are not taped onto main stem upward and on toward coiling cut ends. Repeat with second flower on the 22-inch, no. 12 wire.

Tape balance of this flower stem to where first banana leaf is to be joined at six or seven inches below flower throat. Attach banana just below tip of brace on stem and wrap firmly for two inches with Coban. Tape again over Coban with Floratape and continue taping main stem to within last three inches, where it will be joined to the other two stems about eight inches from end of large flower stem.

Place flower at tip of 22-inch length no. 10 wire that has been unbound for six inches in same way as other flower was placed. Tape stem of this heavier flower with Floratape for 10 inches, to point where heavy stem with a banana at each end will be added. Join these two stems with Coban, wrapping on the bias at about 10 inches below throat of flower, and wrap two stems together with Coban to within three inches of end of flower stem. Join first flower with Coban at this point at about three inches from end of first stem. Continue firm wrapping with Coban past end of the joined stems to the throat of the end banana skin. Cover Coban wrappings with firm Floratape.

Set in position slowly and carefully as pictured. Mask leaves and flower with tissue paper and spray stem generally, but not too much, with flat black to darken. Spray lower stem with delphinium and turquoise slightly to pick up leaf shade. Repeat in area of other banana skin on stem. Do not be too exact. Check flower calyx to see if additional red or gold'n'pearl is needed and be sure banana calyxes are de-emphasized with a darkened area.

Cut a hole the size of a dime in a large cardboard to protect flower color from glitter glue spray and spray glue on abutilon pods through this little hole. Sprinkle pod with silver and bright blue glitter dust simultaneously. If you prefer, mix a teaspoonful of half Elmer's Glue-All and half water and dab it gently on to pod form on all sides, then dust with glitter. Excess glitter will blow away as it adheres only over glue.

9. IVY BRANCH

3 medium scotch pine cones
 about 36 glycerined evergreen ivy leaves for flower petal
18 euonymus berries
 6 light bound wires (about no. 28) 16″ long for throating
 2—no. 14 wires about 16″ long, 1—no. 14 wire 11″ long
 1 yard hemp or string
 2 or 3 clamps to hold stemmed end of string while drying
 Elmer's Glue-All, Coban
 floral spray paint: Clearspray or antique gold and silver
 simple branching

 Alternate: glycerined smilax is a rich amber shade and elegant
 with antique gold finish on a rope stem.

Curve bound 16-inch throating wire at four inches from end. Use this curve as center for a one and one-half times twist around the cone, wedging the wire between the two rows of petals nearest stem end of cone. Bring out uneven wires at opposite sides of cone and twist once tightly at cone throat. This leaves one long end of the bound wire and one end about one and one-half inches. Wad one inch of Floratape into a tight pebble. Poke heavy no. 14 stem wire tightly against wad of tape and bottom of cone and twist of first wire. Tape to the no. 14 main wire with twist at throat pinching wires and wad tightly together, keeping tape bias for one-half inch. Wedge a second throating wire into cone between two rows of cone petals just above first throating wire, repeat bringing wires down opposite sides of cone. Twist once tightly between cone bottom and first wire twist and once again below and as close as possible to first wire twist. Adjust all throating wire ends, two short ones and two long ones, so they are parallel with the main stem. Put one or two half-inch wraps of tape at random to keep wires straight as you continue taping the five thicknesses together to within three inches of stem end. Stem another cone on the 16-inch wire the same way. Stem the third cone on the 11-inch wire the same way with one exception. Tape this third stem all the way to the end of the stem.

Unravel hemp to get strands which, when flattened out so that each thread is lined side by side, are no wider than one-half inch. (See string instructions, page 18.)

Wrap first stem with string to within six inches of the end. Coil unused string neatly into about a two-inch package and wire high onto stem to keep it out of the way temporarily. Wrap second stem with string to within three inches of end and coil unused string in same way. Wrap third stem with string for only three inches below the cone throat and coil excess. The plan is to make as few string joinings as possible (preferably none) in the middle of a stem.

Join first stem to second stem with Coban just above where the taping stops on each stem with both cones facing in same direction. Snip away any flocked wire part of the throating on this part of the stem to make a smoother joint. Tape these two stems together for three inches. Uncoil first stem roping and, adding paste, wrap over the three-inch joint. Finish off wrapping neatly, tucking end up and under

Figure 1 (above) Holidaisy Boutonniere—*page 29*

Figure 2 (left) Single-Petaled Honesty
Flower—*page 33*

Figure 3 Honesty Rosette Flower—*page 36*

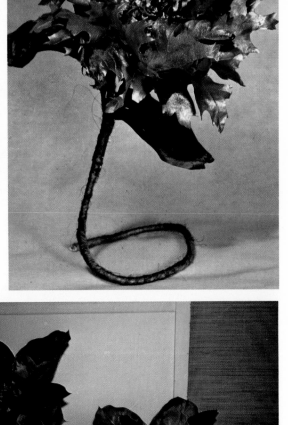

Figure 4 (above) Arborvitae Wallflower—
page 48
Figure 5 (lower right) Rubber Plant set and
plaque—pages 51 and 138
Figure 6 (upper right)
Oak Happy Flower—
page 58

Figure 7   Honesty Candle Spiral —*page 92*

Figure 8   Rainbow Seeds—*page 108*

Figure 9   Raspberry Ripple—*page 72*

Figure 10   Freefall—*page 108*

Figure 11 (above) Iris Pods and Persimmon Calyx "Fretwork" positioned as a base for a candle—*page 109*

Figure 12 (upper right) Iris Pods and Persimmon Calyx "Fretwork" positioned in a Chieko container —*page 109*

Figure 13 (lower right) Mango Petals and Catalpa —*page 114*

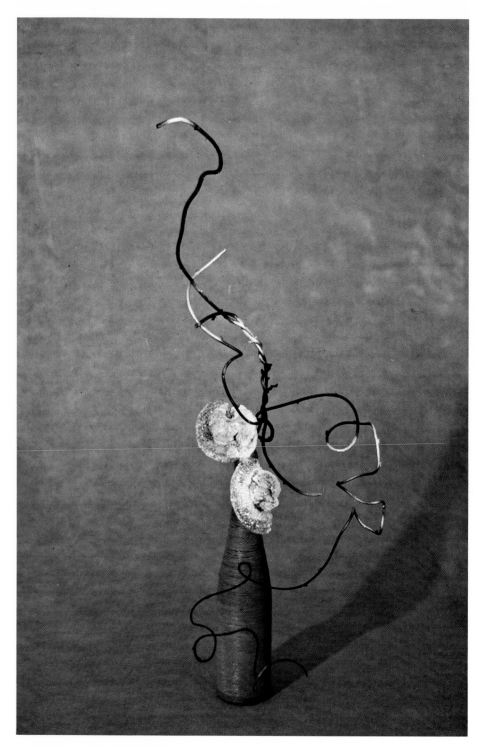

Figure 14   Lichen Ruffles and Wisteria—*page 112*

at least one-half inch of roped end and give end an extra dab of glue. Or if there is enough string left to cover third stem, coil string again to get it out of the way. Attach third stem to the first stem, with cone

placed in same direction as other cone at the point on the third stem where roping stopped just three inches below cone throat. Rope the two stems together firmly and finish roping the rest of the joint and down to the end of the third stem. Glue and clamp all end-of-string sections until dry.

Position set flat on table by coiling end of third stem into a wide C in direction of first stem. Bend, but do not crease, second stem into an upright position. Bend first stem so three bottom inches sit on table top and the rest of the stem stands upright. Adjust so set is balanced for placement of ivy petals. Spray stems with antique gold paint.

Cut stem end point from ends of ivy leaves. Put glue between two bottom rows of cone petals in one cone. Make opposite placements of ivy leaves to form a natural looking flower, unless your ivy is very large leaved. Then make a three-petal bottom row. If this is the case you may have to reshape the stem end of the ivy leaf by cutting a semi-circle to fit in around the cone core. Put glue between next rows of cone petals. Let set. Place this row so no leaf petal is directly over the other and finish with small leaves or let the cone tip show. Paste euonymus berries around center for finish. Repeat with other two flowers. Vary size of flowers if possible, making the shortest stem the medium size flower and the longest stem the smallest flower.

If ivy responds well to glycerin treatment and is a burnished bronze or deep green, a coat of Clearspray is a preservative. No paint is necessary. Otherwise, a light coat of silver and a light overcoat of antique or bright gold makes a good foil for candles. Place in a nest of evergreen branches.

10. SMILAX AND POLYGONUM

about 8 large scotch pine cones, allowing for cutting problems
about 60 glycerined large and small smilax petals
about 4—15″ long multi-twigged branches of polygonum
    after flowering

3—21" lengths ⎫ no. 18 wire for main stems
9— 8" lengths ⎭
    no. 26 wire for stemming cones and polygonum
    brown Floratape, Elmer's Glue-All
    floral spray paints: silver, bright and antique gold
    light wires joined to heavy wire

For this table and candle set tape center five inches of nine eight-inch lengths and six twelve-inch lengths of no. 26 wire. Cut cones carefully in half to leave two layers of cone scales firmly attached to cone core for pasting the petals of the small flowers. The large petals will fit well in the base of the cone.

The tip ends of cone will be throated with one wire. Wrap the taped center of the eight-inch wire tightly one and one-half times around the cone core and bring out on opposite sides of cone. Twist once tightly at stem end of cone. (See cone throating sketches on page 41.) Press an inch of Floratape wadded into tight ball against this twist area, align wires with 21-inch main stem and tape high at the throat to include tape wad, main stem, and throating wires. Continue taping down main stem for four inches. Repeat this on two other 21-inch-length main stem wires and when all three have a tip cone stemmed to one end, attach the stem end split of the cone to the other end of each wire. Place the cut end facing outward from the main stem. This will form the center of the flower when the smilax petals are inserted.

Throat these larger cones with two wires for stability, one long and one shorter wire.

Twist center taped area of an eight-inch length of no. 26 wire one and one-half times around cone between the two rows of cone petals nearest the bottom of the cone. A piece of plain wire will form an opening wedge while you slip the taped wire between the petal rows. Wad one-half inch of tape about the size of a small pebble, press at bottom of cone. Twist wire once at cone throat. Bring throating wires down parallel with stem. Wrap a 12-inch-length throating wire around cone in between next rows of cone petals near cut end. Include wad of tape with throating twist, pinch firmly, and wind one and one-half times around cone. Bring wires out on opposite sides of cone and opposite first wires. Press end of main stem (with tip cone on other end) tightly against and between throating wire twists. Tape five wires firmly for four inches down main stem. Do not let wires twist.

Wire and tape a stem end cut cone on both ends of one eight-inch-length of no. 18 wire. Wire and tape another stem end cut cone on one end of one eight-inch length of no. 18 wire. This will be the candle collar, which is made of one flower with long plumes of polygonum twigs. It is blended with the table design in the picture but it is separate and can be incorporated in the table set as easily as it is set on the candle.

The polygonum branches are made of a series of knotted branchlets which hold the tiny florets. The branchlets are the goal here. They are very durable and can be used without separate wiring where they are not required to bend separately and are joined against heavy wire supports. Crush the fibrous knot just enough to make it "thready" instead of stiff and leave an inch or a little more of stem. Mash the stem somewhat but do not break the branchlet joints. Each branch of polygonum affords seven to 12 knots with feathery-looking durable tips three to six inches long. Cut these branchlets different sizes, being careful to leave enough stem for sturdy throating. Choose the ones with the most twigs and the thinnest throats: 20 to 25 will be easily incorporated. They should be used above and below each heavy wire joint with one or two below each flower to camouflage joint of throating wires and main stem. Some will be wired and stemmed.

Plan three or four lengths of multi-twigged branches five to eight inches long for the candle collar. Tape eight to 10 inch no. 26 wires to coil around the polygonum stems and join to no. 18 wire for the candle collar. When homogenized with the spray paint, they will look like vine tendrils and are better for this purpose than solid taping, which would look bulky. Attach a short and long polygonum branch to both ends of an eight-inch no. 21 wire with a single cone form on one end. Leave two-inch intervals between branch placements.

Stem two long branches with the taped wire coils eight to 10 inches long. Let wire coil around branch and main stem for three inches above stem joint and three inches below, including branch stem. Leave lower two or three inches of coil wire straight to join with main stem wire. Tape knot and straight wire end stem of branch to main stem two inches from other end of main stem and with branch tips extending past end of main stem. Place next branch two inches lower on main stem, continuing tape from previous joint. This keeps tips separate and joints from bumping. Join the remaining eight-inch length of main stem wire which will be a coil wire with no forms attached. Tape two or three inches at both ends and join at end of this taping for two inches to a point where taping stopped beneath cone placement on cone-branch wire. Continue taping this coil wire to untaped area of the wire with branches at both ends until no base wire shows. Curl both ends of this tip coil wire. The set will curve at center joining area and the ends will curl around candle above and below base to hold the collar. The flower form will be at candle base and the twigs will be plumes on either side of the flower.

Stem about 10 polygonum branchlets three to six inches long in the same way described for candle collar stems. Use these stems to camouflage the main stem joints and place after set is assembled.

Tape unstemmed branchlets with crushed knot and stem four inches below each cone placement. Keep tip of branch one and one-half inches below cone. Continue taping on main stems for two inches and place a second unstemmed branchlet on opposite side of each stem directing tip of branch towards cone. Tape six more inches of each main stem after this last addition.

Assemble set. See photographs and sketches for general procedure, pages 93-101.

This is a suggestion only: one or two inches will not affect the style or balance of this size set. The wire affords a malleability that allows for adjustment.

Place three main stems straight and flat on table with tip cones at left and stemmed splits at right and all in line from front to back.

Shift stem closest to you—first stem—four inches to the left. Shift stem farthest from you—third stem—four inches to the right. Join second stem, the one in the middle, with first stem at point two inches to the right of last polygonum joint on second stem. Tape *first* and *second* together toward the right for six inches. Place back on table in original position. Join *third* to *second* three inches to the right of where joint taping ended at last step and tape *third* and *second* together for six inches. Join *fourth* stem at point on third stem three inches to the right of where taping stopped on joint of second and third stem. Attach *fourth* stem by taping the three center inches to third stem.

Position assembly to know where next placement will look best. Bend, but do not crease, center eight inches of spine into a C by pulling spine gently toward you and holding the spine next to bend with other hand. Do not kink. Keep flat on table. Bend six inches at right end toward you. Bend 10 inches at left end slowly away from you and around to right until it forms a C. Bend but do not crease each cone form into an upright position so there is a gentle bottom curve still resting on table where stem is joined to spine. Take stemmed polygonum branches on either side of the main stem joints. Make them of varied lengths so that the low part of the set looks frothy, and place a few extra where needed.

This set can be curved into a tighter circle or a longer linear form. If the area you are planning to adorn calls for an adjustment in shape, make it now so your next placements will do it justice. If you were unusually fortunate with the glycerin treatment of the smilax, this set could be finished with flower petals of a natural brown translucent gold and only the base of the set gilded. The entire set finished in bright white gold is more formal. If you choose natural leaves spray paint now. If entire set is to be gilded, leave paint for last step. (See page 9 for instructions on spray technique.) Spray lightly first with bright gold, then with silver. Be sure the tape is completely disguised. A final casual spray around the base with antique gold will tone down the joint areas. This is not essential as the full flower forms should conceal the base with the help of the frothy polygonum.

Put generous dabs of glue inside cones between cone petal rows. Cut stems from smilax leaves. Use a heavy wire to wedge any reluctant cone petals apart to receive the more tender smilax petals. When glue has set in a few minutes add smilax petals with thought to size. Add glue to each leaf and cut stem end before placing in cone. Make opposite placements each time if the flower is made on a four-petal pattern. The small flowers pictured are made in the tip cones and show placements of three petals in each row.

Whatever your material suggests, let it guide you. Do not overburden the cones. This leaf has a great deal of force and a little goes far. Place flower petals in one flower at a time, choosing the second flower well away from first so as not to jiggle while glue is setting. Be sure polygonum is angled safely away from petals as they drape from the cone in some placements and could be bruised by the branch tips. Be very light-handed with spray paint when painting petals. They must be sprayed from 10 inches away. Make final adjustments before putting away the paint cans. Normal handling will not mark the taped stems but major alterations might show.

11.   EUONYMUS AND POKEWEED

about 80 glycerined small euonymus leaves
3   hemlock cones
12   necklace-like pokeweed pods
2—10″ long no. 21 wires
4— 8″ long no. 21 wires
1—14″ long no. 30 wire
1—12″ long no. 30 wire
1— 3″ long no. 30 wire, bound if available
Elmer's Glue-All, floral spray paints : silver and flat white
white or twig Floratape; if you are going to use on a white
    tablecloth use white Floratape
two two-flower sets are joined here for this "Snow Queen"
    arrangement

alternate : small ivy, glycerined

Cut stems from all but two glycerined leaves. Wash gently with soap and water. This leaf weeps glycerin sometimes. Let dry thoroughly.

Stem three hemlock cones carefully as this is a full load. A small scotch pine could be used but is not quite as effective. Tape two and one-half inches of both ends of 14-inch long no. 30 wire. Tape one end of 12-inch length of no. 30 wire for two and one-half inches. Twist center of taped area of a taped wire end into hemlock cone between two cone petal rows safely near bottom of cone and go around one and one-half times with wire ends coming out on opposite sides. Twist wire once tight at cone throat. Do this on each end of one wire. Repeat on taped end of other no. 30 wire which has one untaped end.

If you have a three-inch piece of fine bound wire, thread the pokeweed rings on each end, pinching in center to keep them from meeting. Put six or seven on each end and let slip down so the end wires can be coiled into an embroidery knot large enough to keep rings from slipping off end of wire. Put one and one-half inch of untaped end of 12-inch long no. 30 wire through pinched loop at base of these ringed hybrid stamen and throat with tape, pinching tape high against bottom rings to keep them firmly superimposed. Tape down along long wire for three inches. Tape over area directly under rings to include a euonymus leaf and stem with the taped wire throat and tape firmly for one-half inch. Add the other leaf with with stem one-

half inch lower to clasp the ringed stems between the two leaves. Tape two 8-inch long no. 21 wires into the throat. Tape all three wires together, keeping them parallel so they do not twist, until the three stems are taped together from throat to throat. Throat carefully under the cone end. Join the two 8-inch length reinforcing wires to the first stem with a cone on both ends and tape the three wires together again, keeping straight and aligned. Complete at each end with careful throating.

Tape the two three-ply stems together by taping the stem with one cone, four inches below the cone for four joint inches, to the other stem below one of the cones so both stems are joined off center. This set can be used in a bowl with fresh spidery greens or a few feathery white sprayed branches. It will adjust to a candle or sit on the table with ease.

Position it to stand by curving center of wire into a semicircle. Adjust flowers so they are different heights with bud form tallest. Conceal base with placement of a large form.

Put Elmer's Glue-All in and around the cone petals. Paste the petals to form the flowers, making opposite placements each time. Do not force petals into cone—use a wire as a wedge. Dribble glue in for each placement.

Spray silver and white paint alternately from 10 inches away, a little at a time, shaking and moving can constantly. (See page 9.)

12. SCOTCH PINE STOLE

30 whole scotch pine cones
12 day lily pods
1—28″ length no. 10 wire } for spine
4—16″ lengths no. 10 wire }
    spool of no. 26 wire
    brown or twig Floratape
    clear spray

Sixty-three whole cones, splits of stem ends, centers, and tips of scotch pine with a few day lily pod clusters for emphasis, are individually stemmed to a spine of no. 10 main wires. These wires are joined in a *simple branching method* so there is no sudden bulk because of reinforcement. Both ends of wire are left free of spine and extended with two or three unequal length tip form stems. A 16-inch-long reinforcing wire is added every six inches to the first half of the design, which is then turned and worked from the opposite end back to the center. The stemming wire weight is no. 26. Brown or twig Floratape is used to cover wire and joints. Materials are grouped to shift visual focus from left to right. Two center splits branched at left of spine are countered by three splits spiraled at the right of spine and three to five small tip end placements accent the motion at irregular intervals.

This stole drapes a lintel, a door, dinner table, or mantel with equal vigor and grace. It holds level when lifted but can be curved into a patterned wreath. There is a matching candle accessory in the next photograph.

Stem about 25 splits each of tip and bottom ends, 10 small whole cones and 12 day lily pods. Use 12 inches of taped no. 26 wire throating cone in center of wire and taping doubled stem to make an approximately five-inch stem. The cut side of the stem end split makes a form different from the stem end. Throat some one way and some the other for variation. Some stems will be cut shorter. None needs to be longer. Throat the lily pods with a wire drawn through throat as close as possible to stem, and cover with tape using same wire lengths as for cones (see illustration). Tape two inches at both ends of four 16-inch lengths of no. 10 wire. Use one 28-inch no. 10 wire to start and tape one very short stemmed tip cone to end of first main wire with tape. From here on bear firmly in mind that this design is effective because each form is clearly articulated and although cone parts may touch each other they should not crowd each other.

Tape two tip end stems together so cone of second is shorter than cone of first and apply to main stem wire with tape just below first placement. Continue taping main stem to next placement each time. Make a three-stem branch of tips and attach to main stem two inches lower on stem swinging to side opposite previous placement. Tape a two-stem branch of stem end splits, cut side, for the next placement, with second stem placed so the cone will not hit the first stem. Repeat this branch and tape three inches farther down main stem. Add a short-stemmed stem end cone to end of a 16-inch wire and tape the two heavy wires together leaving the first two inches of the heavy wire just added as a free stem. Continue making varied placements in this fashion for another five inches.

Keep balancing in your hand as some cones are heavier than others, depending on age and dampness, and these recommendations are only estimates. If you do not need the fifth heavy wire do not use it. Be sure to continue taping entire stem of each placement to main stem spine, which is now composed of two heavy wires, and tape all the way each time to the next placement. The tape adds strength. Keep the joined wires parallel to the spine and do not let them twist. As

you continue branching, plan fuller groups toward center and inter-
sperse their heaviness with branches of two or three tips or two or
three lily pods. As you come to the end of a main wire after the
halfway mark, leave two to six inches of it free from spine and finish
it with tip materials for relief. Spine wires can be cut shorter or
omitted as you proceed and achieve confidence. This can be a permanent possession and is worth doing with that in mind. Apply clear
spray when finished. Green branches or beige ribbonlike grasses are
a fine background.

This branching is effective with any kind of material. The composition may vary but the simple method is a fine showcase for climax
materials.

Background: Tatami

13. SCOTCH PINE CANDLE SPIRAL

18 cone forms are used on two no. 10 spine wires

See Scotch Pine Stole for method (page 88) and photograph (page 91).
Background: chestnut wall, slate table top, copper stick and dish.

14. HONESTY CANDLE SPIRAL

(Shown in color, Figure 7)

3 hemlock cones
    about 30 outer seed petals of honesty for flower form. Dry away
    from light to keep green as in picture or they will turn beige.
    The inner seed pod petal is white and makes a good alternate.

   4   glycerined medium size leucothoe leaves or glycerined large
         andromeda leaves
   1–38″ length no. 26 wire } for main stems
   1–26″ length no. 26 wire }
   1–18″ length no. 21 wire } for reinforcing
   1–11″ length no. 21 wire }
   2–12″ length no. 26 wire } for leaf stems
   2– 3″ length no. 26 wire }
         brown Floratape, Elmer's Glue-All, antique gold spray paint

Tape center four inches of 38-inch wire. Tape *one* end of this wire for three inches. Both of these taped sections will now throat a hemlock cone and the 38-inch wire will be doubled and taped together eventually to form one stem with a cone at both ends.

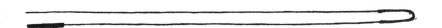

Wedge the taped center section of the 38-inch wire gently between two rows of hemlock cone petals near bottom of cone. Pry the petals apart enough to pull the taped wire one and one-half times around the cone securely and bring extended ends of wire down on opposite

sides of cone to stem end of cone. Twist tightly once, pinching cone and wire with one hand while tightening with the other. This puts the stress on the wire instead of on the tender cone. Tape this area of twist high under bottom of cone and down the stem for one-half inch, pinching the twist tightly to minimize the bump. Throat a hemlock cone in the center of the taped area of the taped end of the doubled light wire. The amount of wire used to twist around the cone just wired will make the matching end of the wire about one inch too long to be joined at this cone throat. Cut off the approximate excess one inch from the untaped wire end and join with the cone wire at twist area. Tape high under throat for one inch. Join the two wires with 18 inch no. 21 reinforcing wire to this throat joint. Tape all three wires together for four inches keeping wires parallel. This will be called the *main stem*. Press the 18-inch length no. 21 reinforcing wire

tightly against this twisted throat area after cutting excess so all three wires fit from cone throat to cone throat without buckling, and tape again over the first throatings. Continue taping down stem for four inches, keeping the two thin wires together and aligned with the heavy wire. Do not let the wires twist. For temporary control of the doubled light wires and the heavier reinforcing wires until set is assembled, tape these three wire thicknesses together for one inch at random intervals along this tripled stem. This prevents twisting.

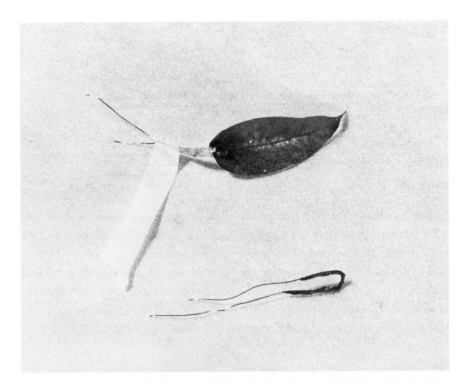

General stages of assembly for a 7 form set

Tape center four inches of 26-inch wire. Tape *each* end of this wire for two inches. This wire also will be doubled to form one stem with a leaf on one end and a cone on the other.

Throat a hemlock cone in the center taped area of the 26-inch length wire and repeat procedure followed in taping of previous two cones, adding the 11-inch-length reinforcing wire at the twist under the throat and taping down the tripled stem for four inches. Do not

twist stem wires. Form each of the taped ends of this wire into a loop, centering loop in center of the two inch taped area. This will be the front and back brace of a leucothoe leaf. (See double loop instructions on page 22.)

Cut away thickened one-eighth-inch *end* of stems of leucothoe leaves. Tape a leucothoe leaf between the two hairpinlike loops just formed at the end of the last wire, which has a cone on the other

end. Tape so that only one-quarter inch of loop brace shows on front and back of leaf above the leaf stem joint. Tape for a half inch, including four wire thicknesses of loop and the natural leaf stem, and press free end of 11 inch reinforcing wire onto this taped stem leaf joint. Tape over joint tightly to include the reinforcing wire and continue tape down stem for four inches. Pinch leaf firmly between front and back loop so braces conform to leaf. This stem with a leaf at one end and a cone at the other will now be called the *second stem*.

Tape the two end inches of both of the 12-inch long no. 26 wires. Loop these taped ends with loop in center of taped area. These two wires will form another double stem with a leaf braced on both ends between the looped ends of the wires. Place a leaf between two end loops and press leaf, stem, and loop ends, firmly with just one-quarter inch of braces resting on leaf above leaf stem joint. Tape leaf stem and loops down double stem wires for four inches. Repeat with another leaf pressed between the other two end loops. This doubled stem with a leaf at both ends will be called the *third stem*.

Tape center inch of the two remaining three-inch wires and form leaf brace for the remaining leucothoe leaf. Tape stem for one and one-quarter inches below leaf stem joint and, without tearing tape, apply to second stem four inches below cone end of second stem with tip of leaf facing toward cone. Tape slightly over end of previous taping on second stem and tape leaf stem and second stem together toward center of second stem for four inches. This leaf should now extend from second stem with its own stem of a little more than one inch.

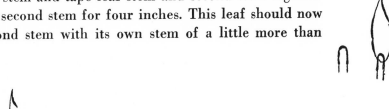

General procedure in joining stems of set

Join third stem, with a leaf at both ends, to main stem with a cone at both ends. Tape center four inches of third stem jointly with main stem starting the joint about four inches below cone on main stem just above where main stem taping stopped. Tape third and main

stems together from this point down toward other end of main stem for four inches. Do not twist stem wires. Pinch as you tape to keep a tightly wrapped stem.

There is a distance of about nine inches from this last joint to the cone on the other end of the main stem. Join second stem to main stem so leaf end of second stem extends from main stem with a leaf stem of about two inches. Join at the bottom end of this two-inch stem to main stem slightly above where previous taping stopped on main stem. Continue taping main stem and second stem together toward center of main stem for about five inches or until there is one inch of main stem free between this joint section and the last joint. All wires should now be taped so no wire is showing and all tape smoothed firmly.

With the assembly now complete except for honesty petals to be placed in hemlock cones, it is well to position it so placement of petals can proceed. Put assembly flat on table with main stem line fairly straight from left to right. It measures about 17 inches. Form an S curve of center five inches of main stem flat on table. Bend but

Assembled skeleton for a 7 form set

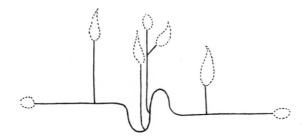

do not crease the stems on both ends of the S into an upright position, grasping firmly at bend area to keep from kinking or twisting. Articulate the leaves and cones so the cones face upward and the leaves extend in graceful natural attitudes. There are seven forms in this set and at least 49 ways to make it balance. Whatever works for you is the right way to do it.

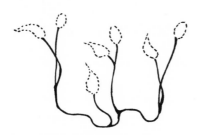

Spray antique gold paint lightly on stems, calyxes, and leaves to blend tape and mechanics. Only the tip of the cone will show to advantage if left natural. It is also pretty with antique gold highlighting it. If you prefer it to be brown, tuck a small piece of wet paper around top of cone or tape a coil of paper around it but leave calyx exposed to the spray paint. Handle lightly when dry so as not to rub spray paint off Floratape.

Position honesty petals. (For details, see Single-Petaled Honesty Flower, page 33.)

Dribble glue deep between cone petal rows at low part of cone and let set for a few minutes. Place petals opposite each time to form flower. Let dry.

When completed and thoroughly dry, twist once around candlestick at point where stem has no joint. Place flowers and leaves to communicate and reach out. The next time you do this it will be simpler.

15. *CANDLE JABOT*

       about 48 southern pine cone petals
       about 30 agave pods
    1—18″ length ⎫
    1—16″ length ⎪
    1—10″ length ⎬ no. 18 wire
    1— 8″ length ⎭
       no. 30 wires for stemming agave pods
       no. 26 wires for stemming cone petals
       Elmer's Glue-All, absorbent cotton, knife, clothespin
       brown or twig Floratape
       floral spray paints: Clearspray, gold'n'pearl

Texture and form assist this arrangement but directional place-ment gives the thrust to this simple design. Agave pods grow in an open cluster and are a fine oval with a satin texture. The dull blunt vigor of the southern pine cone petal makes a happy union. Direc-tional placement and simple branching are the methods used. The jabot is started at what is the bottom in the picture. This design can stand upside down with the ring that holds it around the candle as a base. It is elegant on a wooden candlestick with Clearspray and twig Floratape. Gold 'n' pearl spray is used in the picture.

Soak cut ends of cone petals in a small dish for one hour to soften. Wedge knife into cut edge and pry top layer loose from lower layer. See sketch on page 56. Shape cut end sides to a slant so a narrow throating can be made. It is easy to cut when wet and split.

Wire the agave pod as near as possible to bottom of its throat. Poke holes with fine needle, then thread taped no. 30 wire through holes and use only three and one half inches of wire to make a small fine calyx. There is no weight to the pod and the tape will clinch to the taped wire as long as it did not break the pod when threaded through. If this is not feasible, try poking a fine bound wire in after using needle first and using an embroidery knot twist. See sketches on pages 21 and 22. Tape throat and three inches of stem.

When cut petal ends are layered, the peeled top layer may be thready but, pasted to the cotton and wire, will dry firm. Insert a wire hairpinlike loop by bending a four-inch wire one and one-half

inches at one end and tucking loop inside of petal for three-eighths of an inch with a wisp of gluey cotton for an assist. Clamp with a hair curler or clothespin until dry, then tape throat, including first quarter inch of end of petal and down the stem for three inches. Each of these 80 pieces now has its own stem.

Tape an agave pod to the end of the longest no. 18 wire, which is 18 inches. Tape a cone petal on both sides, allowing one inch of stem free for taping. Make each petal placement so it is no longer than the throat of the previous placement. This ribbony look comes from a directional placement. Note from the picture how the agave pods are swirled in the center and the cone petals swirl parallel with the pods. Tape a petal on top of a pod toward the left and one inch below. Tape another petal at same interval toward the right. Repeat with an agave pod and so on for three repeats.

Add an agave pod to end of 16-inch-length of no. 18 wire and join to first heavy wire with a petal placement; add another petal and now put in a branch. A branch is two or more stems joined to each other but not bunched. Place a petal so tip is over lower third of another petal and tape the two stems together with an inch of the stem free on second petal. Join this stem in the center of double main wire. Stem another branch pair and add swinging to same side. Join two more branches and tape to main stem farther away from side on which they are pointed and again point in same direction as previous branches. This is a diagonal grouping. Join the 10-inch wire here, taping a branch of two short-stemmed agave pods to tip of the heavy wire, taping it very firmly to other main wires. Follow with another branch of agave and then with a single cone petal swinging to alternate sides, then a pair of petals again alternate. Measure your composition and add the last main reinforcing wire to come out about even with another heavy wire. It will be the coil end to clasp the candle. Add three petals in switch direction when you reach the end. Continue in this way more or less until you are out of material or out of wire. It is all malleable but strong enough to stand on its own three-inch-diameter coil or hang as pictured with the cone petals stemmed tightly to the three-inch-end coil so no wire shows. Leave only a quarter inch of stem free with those last three petal placements.

16. CANDLE SET
MAHOGANY AND BOTTLEBRUSH POD PAIR

20 mahogany pods
20 bottlebrush pods
no. 18 bound wire, 10 ten inch and 10 eleven inch lengths
no. 22 bound wire, 10 ten inch lengths
floral spray paint: Christmas red, gold'n'pearl, bright gold
needle, drill

A design made in pairs or groups has many possibilities. Made on the *two flower set* principle in the simplest assembly method, this is easily adapted from the position illustrated: for a pair of candles

with one collar for each, for a candle collar and table set, or for a mantel or doorway with several sets intertwined and used against a background of fresh yew. Other climax material could be substituted. Choose contrasting forms; a round with a linear or a fat one with a flat one.

Dampen bottlebrush pods so they will not break when pierced. Set aside.

Drill two opposite holes at tip end of mahogany pod. Drill two more opposite holes just above the first two. Repeat with the other 19 mahogany pods. Pull about three inches of the 10 inch length no. 18 wire through first holes so both ends extend from same side of pod. Pull ends back up through loop on opposite side and bring down. Repeat on other end of this wire with another mahogany pod. Pull 11 inch length of no. 18 wire through upper holes so wire comes through pod on opposite side from first wire. Repeat on other end of this wire. Twist wires tightly at throat, two wires at a time, at both ends. Tape stems for four inches from high under throat.

Puncture two holes near stem end of bottlebrush pods. Pull three inch end of no. 22 wire through so ends come out on hollow side. Pull ends back up through loop on opposite side and bring down very gently as this pod is more fragile than the mahogany pod. Twist once and throat with tape as high as possible under throat. Tape stem for four inches. Repeat on other end of this wire. Make nine more double ended single stems with bottlebrush pod at each end.

Tape a bottlebrush pod stem to a mahogany pod stem at each end for one and one half inches so bottlebrush extends one inch past mahogany on one end, and is just short of the mahogany on other end. Do this until five stems result, each having four placements. Tape inch and one half of each four stems to one stem, each joining close to a previous joint. Join each stem so stem lengths will vary. Repeat this assembly for the second set. A faint coat of Christmas red floral spray paint, overdusted with gold'n'pearl gives a dull rich woody look. Highlight with bright gold.

To position as a candle trim, form S curve base and place around base of candle or candle-stick, concealing stems as much as possible. Articulate each form facing forward and up.

17. *FREEFALL*

(Shown in color, Figure 10)

This composition sits, stands, stretches, or floats.

Poppy seed tops of different sizes are sliced from the poppy seed cup. Burdock burrs — one or two piggy-back — and glycerined sweet-fern leaves are branched at random but grouped for emphasis.

The textures and forms suggest crewel work. Use no. 30 wire and additional pieces added toward center for stability. The paint is silver, oversprayed with bright gold and touches of Christmas red, and the burrs are dusted with silver, red, and gold glitter dust.

Background: gold and silver paper.

18. *RAINBOW SEEDS*

(Shown in color, Figure 8)

Glycerined sweet-fern petals are glued in cones branched with polygonum twigs. Taped no. 26 wire affords lightness, mobility, and balance. The sweetfern is maneuvered forward and the bright twigs hang to the back. The sweetfern puffs are red, blue, silver, and green, with silver and gold and matching glitter dust. The polygonum twigs are silver and gold with silver and gold glitter. The design is hung on its own stem, curved into a hook at the end with a nylon thread swinging hanger.

6 *Arrangement Variations*

1. IRIS PODS AND PERSIMMON CALYX

(Shown in color, Figures 11 and 12)

about 51 pond flag or iris pods
about 25 persimmon calyxes
5–21″ lengths ⎫
2–12″ lengths ⎬ no. 18 wire
38–9″ lengths no. 26 bound or taped wire
Floratape, twig or green, needle for piercing pods
floral spray paint: gold'n'pearl, bright gold
   the two flower set principle

alternates: any durable pods of similar form

Make about 38 sets of nine-inch-length bound wires with a persimmon pod at each end, a flag pod at each end, or one of each at each end. The bound wire will go through holes on either side of flag pods just above the stem end and the bound wire will also go through a center hole in the persimmon calyx. Pierce pods and persimmon

Figure 15   Sugar Pine Cone Flower and Gum Ball Stabile—*page 120*

Figure 16 Leucothoe Recurved Flowers
—*page 116*

Figure 17 (above) Cowbane Mobile,
"Outreach"—*page 121*

Figure 18 (left) Almost Abstract Fern
Stalk Tree—*page 127*

Figure 19 Cowbane and Coconut Bark in a Sogetsu container—*page* 120

Figure 20 (above) Silent Night Tree
—*page 126*

Figure 21 (upper right) Artemisia
Great Tree—*page 128*

Figure 22 (lower right) Double Artemisia Tree—*page 132*

Figure 23   Sensitive Fern Christmas Tree—page 122

Figure 24 (left) Pignon Porcupine with Tassel—*page 145* Artemisia Puff Treelet—*page 134* Stephanandra Kissing Ball—*page 146*

Figure 25 (above) Fishtail Palm Medallion—*page 141*

Figure 26 (left)   Panel of Cassia and Bignonia
—*page 137*

Figure 27 (below)   Twin plaques, Akebia and Yucca—*page 138*

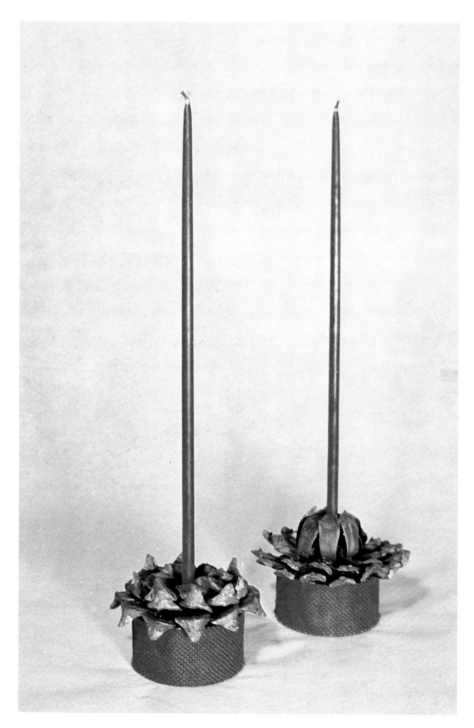

Figure 28   Petaled Candle Holders—*page 152*

calyxes with a needle of the exact size of the wire. Stem the flag pod by drawing one inch of wire through from side to side of pod and bending back to long end of wire. Tape this to wire throat firmly from base of pod for two inches. No twist is necessary. Stem the persimmon by poking end of this two-inch wire up through center hole and extending wire for two inches. Coil one inch of wire around itself into an embroidery knot and tape at throat to keep wire clinched. Each stem now has two heads.

Tape one or two iris pods to end of one main wire *so tips are at least one inch lower than throat of previous placement.* Continue this practice throughout the assembly. The lacy character of fretwork is created by space and upturned placements which would be ruined if the material looked crowded. Tape one or two iris pods at end of each of the main wires.

Each placement will be made by taping some part of the central area of the two-headed stems and each stem will be made longer or shorter in this manner. This makes it possible to use half the volume of supporting wire that would be necessary if the design were made up of individually branched stems.

Bend each stem into a C as you join it to main stems. Do not adjust them until you are finished with a section. If you make each placement one and one-half inches away from the previous one you will be able to do anything you like at the end of the composition but constant twisting will loosen the tape, so be patient. Continue taping after each placement, including main wires, to the point of next placement.

Tape the second main wire to the first at about six inches below the tip of the first wire. In this picture there are two pairs of forms on first wire before second is joined. One stem is added at the joining point each time a main wire is added. Tape two inches farther down and join a third main wire. Add two more stems and one inch farther down join another main wire. Be sure main wire taping is firm. This is the point where two main wires are divided from the other two man wires for the open section and it is effective if one side of this division is emphasized by using only pods for the first six inches. There are about six more stem placements to make before the separated wires are rejoined on this side. Place about eight stems on the other divided wire, starting back at point of division and taping firmly again before adding stems.

Tape separated wires together again, taping main wires so no bare point shows, and add two stems one at a time with a short stem at blossom ends of stems. This hides the next placement. Add a 12-inch main wire here and one or two stems. Add the last main wire, taping it for two inches, *in the center*, to the rest of the other main wires. Join two stems at this center taping area while making the main stem joint. Use short blossom ends again to conceal joint. Tape last main wire starting from each end and use more tip than blossom forms at the end. This will use about 10 stems.

Spread the divided area for about six inches in center. Bend upward left of center so divided area forms two spread supports for tip. Let other end run lazily along the table and bend the last eight inches upright. Position the blossoms so they are all individually expressive, looking up and out at slightly different angles. Apply gold 'n' pearl floral spray paint lightly and from a distance to blend the green tape and bound wire. A discreet touch of bright gold at the tips and on a few of the flowers is a nice highlight.

This would be lovely with many easily throated forms. It is necessary to have a riffled round form and something spiky to create this rhythm. The line and accent of the grouped linear forms show to unusual advantage combined with irregular round forms that have no bulk.

Use with a candle as a table set, arranged in a Chieko container (see Figure 12).

2. *LICHEN RUFFLES AND WISTERIA*

(Shown in color, Figure 14)

2 lichen clusters from a birch tree, spray painted with silver,
       delphinium, and turquoise and matching glitter dust
     wisteria vine spray painted flat black and silver
2—no. 14 bound wires, 1—10″ and 1—14″ long
4—no. 18 wires bound or taped 8″ long
     Coban Elastic Bandage

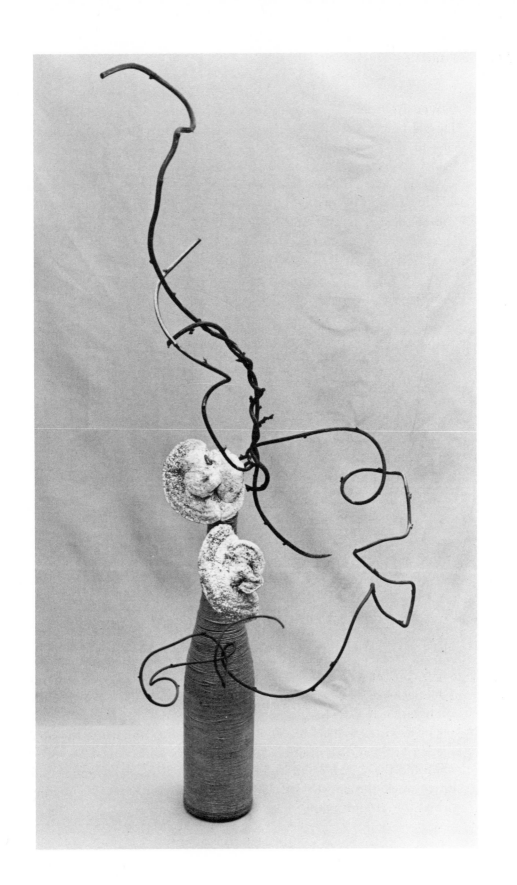

Wet the thick lichen joint to pierce with needle or no. 18 wire. Thread bound wire through four holes, bringing wire out on opposite sides to be joined for security. Tape wire to fit a tight throat, pad with Coban bandage cut to one-inch width to get bulk for transition of throat to lichen. Join a no. 14 main stem wire 10 inches long to one lichen and 14 inches long to other. These forms are positioned with long diagonal forward thrust. Two lengths of wisteria vine naturally intertwined are the upright line and one long spiraled vine comes farther forward than the lichen to frame space.

3. *MANGO PETALS AND CATALPA*

(Shown in color, Figure 13)

2   yucca pods
3   mango pods (dampened and split for six forms)
7   catalpa pods curled naturall, 3 partly open
3   long sweet cicely stalks
12—no. 18 bound wires, 12″ long
    no. 26 plain wire for Floratape throating
1—12″ length bound wire
    floral spray paints: aluminum, delphinium blue, antique gold

Yucca pods are stemmed on 12 inches of flocked wire through two holes in stem end. Do not cut edges of the mango pod. The hairy look is more effective than a cut, man-made edge. Two 12-inch lengths of bound wire are used for each split, threaded in center through pod in opposite directions. (See Candle Set and Table Form on page 106.) The yucca will be the center of a group of bound wires, throated together to form each flower. (See embroidery knot, page 22.)

Spiral a three-inch bound no. 26 wire, bend in a V at center and slip through throat wire in center of yucca pod before tightening wire at throat and taping. This forms stamen.

Mango pod splits should be pierced with four holes near pointed stem end. A bound no. 18 wire is threaded through one pair of holes in one direction and one in opposite direction, with end of one wire spiraled to form a calyx and the others taped into the four-ply stem. Tape mango to yucca one stem at a time to throat flower.

Sweet cicely stalks are used for the main and accessory positions. Catalpa pods are pierced at end and wired through to holes with three-inch stems, then taped and fitted into proper lengths of sweet cicely stalks. The tallest stalk is 21 inches. The longest bottom stalk is eight inches. Depth is suggested by placing tall stalks in needle-point holder, one behind the other and by positioning low stalks in same fashion.

Use antique gold paint spray for stem and throat and delphinium blue in the smooth inside of the mangoes. A quick coat of silver clouds the blue and the result is gray pearl. Container is modern pewter, antiqued dark gray, nine inches tall.

4. *LEUCOTHOE RECURVED FLOWERS*

(Shown in color, Figure 16)

The glycerined leucothoe flower is made on a tip end of a southern pine cone with three rows of cone petals. It is about two inches long. It is attached to a no. 14 main stem wire with taped no. 26 throating wire. (See pages 8 and 52.)

There are 25 petals in each flower. A poppy seed top sliced from bottom cup of pod is glued to cut end of cone.

A scindapsus vine naturally twisted has been looped with both ends inserted in a pinholder so the main line of the design frames space. No paint is used. The container is stoneware.

5. SMILAX IN WALL

6   small scotch pine cones for flower base
32   glycerined smilax leaves of varied sizes for flower petals
1—30″ and 2 or 3 shorter glycerined smilax vines with leaves naturally
     attached
12—10″ lengths of no. 30 wire for throating (2 wires for each
     flower form)
3—12″ lengths no. 18 wire for main stems
     brown Floratape, Elmer's Glue-All
     floral spray paint: antique gold, copper

These smilax flowers are made in small scotch pine cones each throated with two taped no. 30 wires to opposite ends of a main stem of no. 18 wire 12 inches long. After a cone is throated and attached to main stem at one end of each of the two main stem wires, a third main stem is added for reinforcing. All these wires are then taped into one tripled stem with a cone at each end of the stem. (See Two Flower Spikenard on page 61.) The stem and cone are spray painted with antique gold. After petal placements are made, the whole is oversprayed with copper spray paint.

6. *THE COBWEB, OR FOUR ON THE FLOOR*

The friendly aspect of the common house spider is that he makes an irregular web. He does not become ensnared because he knows which threads he has rendered sticky.

A spool of no. 30 light gold wire was used to construct this free-hanging fancy. The general diameter is about 12 inches. It is stretched, puffed and curved so as to give an illusion of depth. Create a circle of the wire and keep the wire continuous, making about eight radii into the center, then weaving the wire with a full twist around each radius to complete a circle within outer rim. Develop wide circles near outer rim first. Repeat by making smaller circles around the radii as you move toward center of web. Keep the spool tightly coiled as you work and it will thread in and out very easily. Four amateur spiders took to the floor to hold the wire circle in shape while a fifth wove the web. The butterfly has wings of lichen petals, the body is a flag pod, and stems are used for antennae.

The spider's body is an Indian cup calyx and its legs are made of knotty polygonum twigs. The eyes are the seeds of a beech burr.

The bee is a black-eyed Susan center with under wings of milkweed pod membrane.

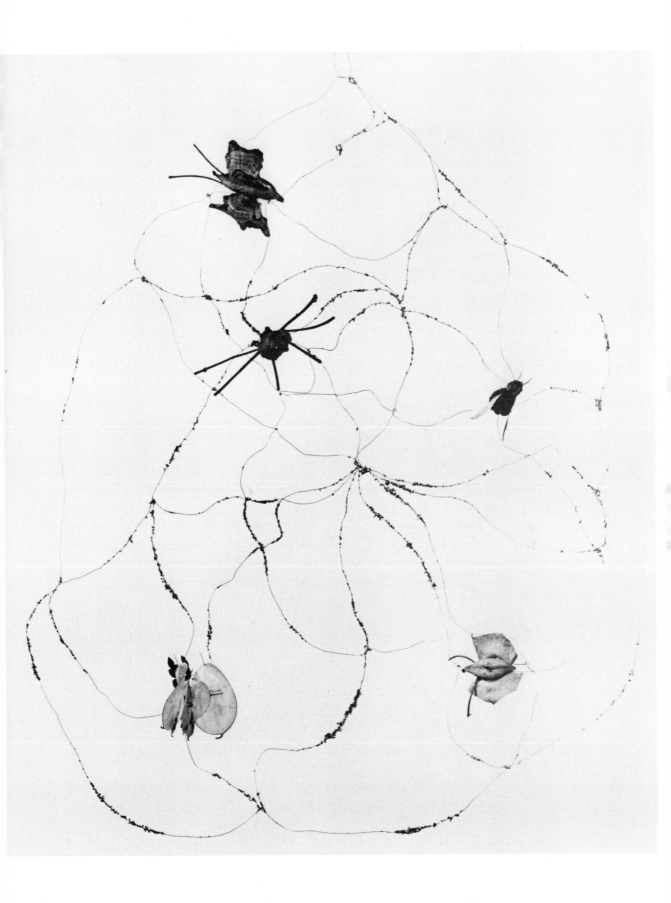

The honesty wings of the moth below support a body of sweet-fern leaves.

A Canterbury bell seed pod and wings of broken persimmon calyx form the grubby fluff opposite.

Stretched into a corner and hung so it is attached in two places, instead of swinging free, it can become a permanent companion.

7. *SUGAR PINE CONE FLOWER AND GUM BALL STABILE*

(Shown in color, Figure 15)

8 sugar pine cone petals
5 gum balls: 2 for flower centers, 3 hanging on nylon thread
  smilax vines
  Indian cup square stem

Gum balls are drilled through from side to side to be wired in center of flower attached to main stem. The pine petals are stemmed with bound wire inserted in slit of petal and wires are then throated and stemmed together. The completed four inch flower stems are then inserted in hollow stems. See sketch, page 21 and photograph.

The gum balls are spray painted Derusto fluorescent red. The cone petals and smilax vine are spray painted flat white.

8. *COWBANE AND COCONUT BARK*

(Shown in color, Figure 19)

Seed pods have been cut from the ends of the blossom skeleton of cowbane and two cuplike parts are wired to each other through the stem end with glue for reinforcement. The throated wire is fitted into the pulpy center of the square Indian cup stem.

Bleached coconut bark is cut on the grain for leaves. Green Derusto fluorescent spray paint is used with silver and blue glitter dust.

9. COWBANE MOBILE, "OUTREACH"

(Shown in color, Figure 17)

Derusto fluorescent green spray paint, silver and blue glitter dust
Elmer's Glue-All

Winged seeds have been cut from the ends of cowbane umbels which are sewn together throat to throat and hang on nylon thread from no. 18 stick wire. The top bar measures about 18 inches.

7 Tomorrow Trees

1. SENSITIVE FERN CHRISTMAS TREE

(Shown in color, Figure 23)

60 to 80 fertile fronds of sensitive fern. See picture on page 5
1—27″ strip of ¾″ seasoned wood, 1-1½″ wide
1— 2″ strip of the same width and thickness for mini-tree
    about 12″ of green bound wire or 2 prepasted canvas picture
      hangers
1⅔ yards moss green flocked ribbon ¾″ wide
    glitter dust: dark green, light green and silver
    glitter glue
    green fluorescent spray paint
    Elmer's Glue-All, masking tape
    a heavy duty staple gun, optional
    a linear block of wood about 4″ x 8″ or the equivalent to weight
      fronds while glue sets
    1 or 2 deep round pans or tin candy boxes for shaping fronds
      while wet

This tree is effective in all sizes as long as the height-width ratio is constant. Scale it so that the total width of the bottom branches measures less than half the height of the stick of wood on which the tree is based. This tree is 27 inches tall with the lowest branch spread of 13 inches and a three-inch spread at top of stick.

The sensitive fern fertile frond tip has a puffed beaded side showing very little stem. This will be called the right side and is the side facing you. The other, or underside, is relatively flat and pastes well when weighted to dry.

Submerge fronds in water for five or ten minutes until they are sufficiently malleable to curve inside a roasting pan or candy box about 12 to 14 inches in diameter. Do not worry if a few stalks break as many of the placements will be cut with very little or no stalk. Place fronds inside pan right side up, curving them gently around inside rim, three or four at a time. Place half of them going in one direction and the other half, also right side up, going in the reverse direction to create properly curved branches for both sides of the tree. Drain any excess moisture. Dry in container overnight or hasten drying with gentle heat such as on a covered radiator.

A proper handling device or hanger is an essential first step for hanging designs. Sand rough edges of sticks for large and mini-trees and fit with hangers. A prepasted canvas picture hanger can be trimmed not to show behind the trees and, with additional glue, will work well if tied in place with a wire or string close to the top of the tree and left to dry. Remove string or wire before pasting fern tips.

If you use a wire hanger, any wire strong enough to support and fine enough to conceal will do. Bound green wire, blending with the tree, is used in the picture. Make two holes on each stick three-quarters of an inch apart in center of stick one-quarter inch below top. Pull ends of wire from back to front, pulling back loop just high enough to be seen behind the stick from the front. Bend each wire end over to the side nearest the hole on the front of the stick and carry around side of stick to below back loop. Pull up under loop at outer edge on each side. Again lace each wire end close to first wrap on loop at back, keeping twists far enough apart so there is just one thickness of twist behind stick and pull ends down straight on back of stick. Cut off more than one inch excess on both wire ends. Use same process for the large tree stick and the mini-tree stick. This wiring system minimizes the strain on whatever material is pasted on the front of the stick when design is handled.

Form tree. If you have a staple gun you can staple the first two layers of placements. Plot the silhouette of the tree by placing 6 to 10 long downward swooping stems on the stick of wood, anchoring with small pieces of masking tape which should be peeled away before stapling as the wood offers a better bond for the glue, which is used for top placements. Cut the ends of the stems away where they do not conform to the tree shape. (Save all stem ends for Almost Abstract Fern Stalk Tree design on page 127.)

There will be at least two layers of stem or tip superimposed on these initial placements and it is neither desirable nor necessary to build up bulk. A natural puff in the material gives the design all the dimension it needs if you keep in mind the deep hanging attitude of the tree in the picture and make all placements so that the branches at the top of the tree hang over the branches beneath them. Do not fill in all points of the silhouette with the first placement as an irregular approach will add to the depth of the design. Place stalks slanting downward from tree tip at about a 70-degree angle. Using the top of the stick for 12 o'clock, angle each placement downward to about four o'clock. Check with the picture from time to time. After having used most of the stick surface for stapling, begin with gluing as additional stapling may break the initial placement. Apply glue generously and let set for at least 10 minutes before placing additional material.

With or without a staple gun, start the tree by running an eight-inch thick, one-half inch wide column of Elmer's Glue-All down center of stick. It will take fifteen to twenty minutes to set well enough to hold the fern fronds. Apply glue generously with each layer and weight until dry before continuing each time. The top layer of branches is placed more quickly and securely as there is now a larger base which necessitates a little less glue. Each successive layer of feather tip placements, about four or five altogether, extends less far from the tree trunk and no tip should run exactly over the previous one. The distance between each fern tip should vary slightly as it extends from the center—as should the angle of the curled tip. A vertical design gives an illusion of diminishing toward the top and this helps you to make a tree that does not look topheavy. If it seems to have a fairly real look flat on the table you will find this improves when you hang it. Make the bottom area strong and keep the silhouette lacy and slightly irregular. It should be balanced but not exact. It helps to make opposite placements each time.

Make the bottom three to four inches of the stick look like a tree trunk. The root ends you have been cutting have beautifully curved tips which form a romantic finish. Create a trunk on last four inches of tree by pasting seven or eight four-inch-long fern frond ends side by side vertically, with curve at bottom end and rounded side of stem facing front. Let the tips come one-half inch over the bottom edge to conceal the stick edge. Make additional placements of a few brief feathery tips at bottom branch area so trunk seems to come from under the branches. Check top of tree to see that it has a tapered tip extending enough above stick to finish in a point rather than a blunt tip. Let dry overnight.

A mini-tree can be made in the same manner. Let glue set and make placements to extend well beyond top and sides of stick, keeping exaggerated angle of placements. Let dry overnight.

Suggested color combinations using floral spray paint:

> flat white over silver dusted with silver and sapphire blue glitter;
>   blue ribbon
> bright gold over silver dusted with silver glitter; red ribbon
> pale blue and sapphire blue dusted with silver glitter;
>   sapphire ribbon

Green fluorescent spray paint is used in this picture.

These trees are elegant even without ribbon and if you are going to omit the ribbon be sure to give stick end a proper coat of spray when finishing as it will show when tree is hung.

Spray both trees at the same time, placing flat on a large tray or cardboard, with an extra handle on each tree so that it can be turned easily for spraying from all angles. Let dry and repeat from a different angle each time. Keep a distance of at least ten inches from trees, moving and shaking can constantly and spray *lightly and a little at a time* so surface details are not lost in clots of paint. Let dry.

Move to a clean flat surface or box to apply glitter glue with glitter dust simultaneously. (See instructions given on pages 9 and 10.)

Apply the dark green glitter first, sprinkling sparsely, spraying again with glue and sprinkling sparsely again until tree is subtly but generally dusted with the dark green. Jiggle in between dust applications to remove loose glitter dust. Repeat procedure next with light green glitter twice and again with silver glitter. Each process should be repeated each time: glue spray first, dust second, after a minute jiggle and repeat. Hang trees securely on some overhead fixture and dab Elmer's Glue-All on the bottom cut edge or end grain of the stick to let dry for a minute before you thumbtack the ribbon trim on this end of the tree.

Proportion the ribbon to the size of the tree. Pictured is a ribbon about four feet long. It is folded nearly in half with one of the two cut ends about two inches longer than the other. It is again folded off center so loop end hangs two inches shorter than shortest cut end. Place two thumbtacks in off-center fold of doubled ribbon in center of stick. Attach fold to glued end grain of stick at an angle so loop flips over toward side front in front of cut ends. The tips of the trunk will conceal area where ribbon is attached. Repeat on small tree with about 14 inches of ribbon.

When finished hang safely and remove work hanger.

2. SILENT NIGHT TREE

(Shown in color, Figure 20)

Venetian blue sensitive fern frond tree, twenty-four inches long—seven inches wide at lowest branch. Follow instructions for the Sensitive Fern Christmas Tree.

This proportion is styled for narrow panes on sides of doors or white walls with brass accessories. A red ribbon band with narrow dark blue center would be a fine trim.

Use floral spray paints, delphinium blue and silver and silver and the glitter dust.

3. *ALMOST ABSTRACT FERN STALK TREE*

(Shown in color, Figure 18)

About 30 root end tips of sensitive fern fertile frond (residue of the
 Sensitive Fern Christmas Tree design)
About 10 glycerined stephanandra leaves of varied sizes—small
 varied untreated oak leaves can be substituted
8" wood strip ½" thick, ¾" wide
1 no. 214 screw eye about ⅛" eye for hanging or a 6" strip of no. 30
 wire or fine brown cord (the cord is the best choice for handling if
 design is to be used on a table)
Elmer's Glue-All, Q-Tips, sandpaper
brown shoe polish or wood stain
floral spray paints: silver, delphinium blue
glitter dust: silver, bright blue

Sand rough edges of stick. Rough stick front slightly with sandpaper to make glue adhere if stick is not already rough. Polish edges
and sides with shoe polish or wood stain. Do not polish front of stick.

Insert screw eye at top of stick in end grain or make holes for wire
or cord three-eighths of an inch apart and thread wire or cord into
holes as described in Sensitive Fern design, page 122.

Run a one-eighth inch wide by one-eighth inch thick line of Elmer's
Glue-All down center of stick. Let dry five mintues or until nearly
set while you plot your design after studying the picture. Note the
angle at which stems are placed and the random placement. These
stems have a flat side and a round side. The round side has more surface so use it for the front side. This is an uneven balancing of material and the square top and alternate varied spacing create the person-
lity of the Almost Abstract.

Set three or four long stems in glue for first placements to establish
pattern and angle. While waiting for the glue to set, spray the leaves
lightly and at random, first with silver and then briefly with
bright blue, letting them bounce around in the spray box. (See
spray paint instructions, page 9.) Do not spray thoroughly, but casu-
ally. After paint is dry, mix one teaspoon of half Elmer's Glue-All and
half water and dribble on the center spine area of the right side of

leaves, carelessly, so it is not too exact. Then shake glitter, first blue, and then silver on the glued leaves. Let this dry while placing additional fern stem ends to form the tree, dabbing stems with glue at the area that will adhere to the stick. After silhouette is well *suggested* add a few small placements of the tip curled stem ends for emphasis. Clean off excess glue with damp Q-Tip. Dot the wrong side of the sparkled sprayed leaves in one or two places with glue and place small ones oddly near top of tree and larger ones oddly near center and lower branches.

Do other interesting things—a collage or a long interwoven plaque—with the rest of the stem ends as it would be too bad to throw them away.

4. *ARTEMISIA GREAT TREE*

(Shown in color, Figure 21)

28″ seasoned wood strip 2″ wide x ¾″ thick for tree base
250 to 300 flowering form stems of artemisia silver king cut about
      20″ long
  1 yard red satin ribbon 2″ wide
      heavy duty stapler
10″ length of fine wire for ribbon if stapler is not used
  2″ fine needle or pin
      floral spray paints: silver and flat white
      silver glitter dust
      strong nylon thread, no. 212 screw eye for hanging
      sandpaper, large Elmer's Glue-All
      roasting baster ⎫
      a cup with pouring spout ⎭ to apply diluted glue
  2 weight blocks of wood or equivalent, 14″ long x 2″ wide x 1″ thick

Alternate: mustard seed stalks, wild or cultivated, picked for maximum durability while slightly green. These form a more airy, wiry tree dotted with burdock burrs. See end of these instructions for detail.

Artemisia is a naturally durable gray feltlike material suited to mass design. It is equally dramatic scaled to a smaller size. The pictured tree measures 42 inches from its tip to the bottom of the ribbon trunk. The bottom branch spread measures 18 inches. The mini-tree of artemisia on page 134 has been reduced to one-seventh the size of this tree. The wide double tree of artemisia in Figure 22 has a less dramatic silhouette.

Artemisia needs no conditioning if picked after a frost. Do not crush the leaves while gathering as they should remain articulate. The 12-inch flower end of the stem has a beadlike tip which accents the branch line of the tree. The remainder of the dependable leafy stem is used for filler.

If picked before frost it is best to condition for a few days. Cut stems 20 inches long, strip leaves from bottom five inches. Place stems in a container four inches in depth. Maintain a water level of two inches. This allows the stems to spread outward from the top of the container; the leaves will not be too crowded, and the tips will curl.

Material not conditioned and picked after frost can be made to curl at the tip by moistening tips slightly and curving them gently. Prop inside a box corner or basin so the curve is retained after material has dried.

Sand any rough edges of 28-inch stick, which is the tree base. Smooth back, sides, top, and bottom to protect wall or door where it will hang. Some roughness on the front side, which is to be glued and covered with material, is desirable, as it helps glue to adhere. Score front of stick many times with knife or scissors. Place screw eye at top center of stick in end grain wood. This will be the final hanger. Run an extra wire or string through the screw eye to aid in handling during construction and remove when arrangement is finished.

Flow a column of Elmer's Glue-All one-eighth-inch thick and one and one-half inch wide down the center of the stick. Start two inches below top of stick and end at a point two inches above bottom of stick. It will spread to the sides while you are using it. Let glue set to a marshmallow consistency. This takes 15 or 20 minutes. While waiting prepare the stems and plot the silhouette.

A yardstick, string, or folded paper outline, touching the top of the stick and extending to a point eight inches from the side of the stick at the bottom, will guide your placements.

The widest part of the silhouette is established first, by placing opposite branches 12 to 16 inches long at every inch of the stick. Vary the length of the placements slightly but keep the angle constant.

Remove leaves from bottom one and one-half inch of stems so pasting area on stick surface is free for maximum stem-holding accommodation. Each two opposite placements will form an inverted V at the top of the stick as both stem ends start at center of stick and angle away from each other on the diagonal down the stick. Place stems on downward slant with tips curved toward top of tree. Make opposite placements every inch, varying lengths slightly until the stems form a series of inverted V's all the way along the stick to within two inches of the bottom. Each stem should now be secured for one and one-half inches on stick.

Repeat, placing stems opposite at alternate spots between previous placements and varying angle so there is slightly less downward slant where stem is glued to stick. There is now a series of broadened inverted V stem ends all along the pasted stick.

At this stage the glue should be reasonably firm. Staple all the V points and both sides of V's. Few stems should break when they are glue-soaked but the weight of the staple gun should make them firm in the glue even if they do. Apply another column of glue all the way down to within two inches of bottom, including the top two inches this time. Let set. Place leafed ends of stems at same angle as the blossom ends were placed, stripping the leaves from the part of the stem that goes into the glue. Depth and thickness are forming the shape of the tree and the next layer of placements should poke into the little pockets that have formed along the glued stick.

The previous leafy placements will help support these shorter stems, which are now poked into the stick area with the tip ends about three and one-half inches above the table angling into the stick at nearly a right angle. Weight center pasted strip and fill in top area of tree. Leave weighted for a half-hour.

Remove weight and, with an unused stem end, adjust stems, lifting those that may have been pressed down too hard. For the final placements to cover the stick gluing area, use short and long tips and angle them up to tree tip and down and out to bottom. Let some curl across one another slightly. Add each one with glue at stem end and put glue only in stick area to avoid a matted look.

When you are certain the placements are all dry and firm, about an hour later, apply spray paint. (See page 9 for instructions.)

Prop tree at a slant, tying top hook to a box or cardboard longer and wider than tree branches to enable you to spray from the sides and bottom to cover all points adequately. Apply silver floral spray lightly two or three times, letting dry for five minutes in between. Shake and move can constantly and maintain a distance between can and tree of at least eight inches. Repeat procedure with flat white two to four times.

While this is drying prepare diluted solutions of Elmer's Glue-All. Mix half-water and half-glue in cup with pour spout. Stir well and pour into baster. Prop baster safely, and prepare a second cup of same solution so the glitter operation is not interrupted for a refill. Set aside.

Place tree flat on protected surface. Use baster as a syringe. Shake well, sealing tightly with finger, and baste upper half of tree, pumping and spraying to keep solution lightly and thoroughly distributed. The glue should trap the glitter from within the tree depths as well as on the upper surfaces. Spread silver glitter dust generally a little at a time to avoid clots in any one spot. Repeat the glue and glitter on lower half of tree. Let dry five minutes and jiggle gently to make sure enough glitter has adhered. Do not move it until satisfied that it sparkles properly.

Prepare the ribbon for the two-inch bottom area of the stick. Double the yard of ribbon without creasing at the doubling spot which will be a soft loop. Make a loop at cut end of doubled ribbon three and one-half inches long. Pin horizontally. Pull loop down over pinned area and pin again in center of top front loop, which should measure two inches. This forms a pump bow or two even horizontal loops. Stuff loops with rolls of paper. Set aside. Place tree in clean area. Put glue on bottom two inches of tree trunk. Press flat side of pinned loop to glued area. Tie to tree trunk with wire while drying, at very bottom pin which is under long finishing loop of ribbon and at second pinned area between paper-filled loops. If you have a stapler, substitute staple for pins and staple so cleats go in horizontally.

Remove paper rolls and press center crease between loops with fingers so loops stand up and hide creases. Remove wire when glue is dry. Remove work hanger from screw eye and tie with nylon thread if more than screw eye is needed.

Alternate: The mustard seed fronds are multi-branched and make a lacier tree with equal distinction. Without any leaves to build up placements, each stem must be carefully set. Gather them while slightly green so they are not too brittle to handle. The mustard seed is used without curling the tips of the stems and about sixty burdock seeds in varying sizes are placed when tree is finished to look like cones. After the paint is applied the glitter dust is especially directed to the burdock for extra highlights. The burdock burrs are self-adhering but a little extra glue is recommended. An alternate color scheme which will make the tree look more ethereal is bright gold paint over a base coat of silver and silver glitter dust for a finish. A gold ribbon trunk can be substituted for the red ribbon.

5. DOUBLE ARTEMISIA TREE

(Shown in color, Figure 22)

100 to 150 stems of artemisia silver king, blossom stalks 12″ long
1—12″ stick of seasoned wood ½″ to ¾″ thick, 1″ wide, for base of tree
   floral spray paints: delphinium blue, turquoise
   Elmer's Glue-All, glitter glue, glitter dust: delphinium blue,
      bright green, turquoise
   satin ribbons (optional) 24″ long, ¾″ wide, 1 blue, 1 green
   no. 214 screw eye for hanging tree, heavy duty stapler (optional)

   Alternate: coconut palm seed fronds

This frankly fat and happy little tree consists mainly of the delicate beaded tips of the mature flowering form of artemisia. It is broader than it is long and has a dancing air because of its stylized upturned branch tips. (See Artemisia Great Tree, page 128, for instructions on gathering and conditioning, if picked before frost.) The coconut fronds will also dance but will not have the chubby charm of the tree pictured.

Shape the tips of the branches by curling gently into a box corner. The tip ends are very malleable. The cut stem length for this design should be about 12 inches, which allows cuts from short placements to be used for leafy fillers where necessary. This part of the stem is usually malleable enough not to need moistening if fresh. If completely dry, moisten lightly before shaping and let dry before placing.

Place screw eye in end grain of wood at top of stick, carefully centered so the stick will not splinter. Plan now for a support for the tree after the first side is complete. The bottom two inches of the trunk will be made of durable stick ends if you follow the design pictured. Use a 10-inch square box, the sides of which will support the tip of the tree and the wide branch area and trunk, since it is necessary to bear down while stapling or pasting.

The tree is just as effective if you carry the branches the entire length of the stick and use a doubled green ribbon and a doubled blue ribbon thumbtacked to the end grain at bottom of stick for a trunk effect. While you are deciding, place a half inch column of glue one-eighth inch thick down center of stick to within two inches of bottom (see picture) or all the way to the bottom if you are replacing stem trunk with ribbon trunk.

Let the glue set for ten minutes and place outline forms, about six on each side, with leaves removed from the part of stem which is to be pasted across the base stick. Make opposite placements to keep the silhouette in balance. The lowest branch is about eight inches wide and, allowing for the curled tip of stem, this calls for bottom branch stems 10 inches long. About 16 of these will be necessary to do bottom branches of both sides of tree. As soon as glue has set to marshmallow consistency, place opposite branches until entire stick area is pasted. Staple these stem ends onto stick and add another half-inch column of glue. Let set for fifteen minutes.

Place a dozen or more filler stems with leaf only in proportion to silhouette and shorter than underneath branches so that they do not obscure beaded tips of underneath placements. Poke the next short tip stems at an angle into stick area, adding glue to each stem as it is placed, reaching slightly to front of tree and toward you with tips up each time. Let dry for a half-hour before turning over on supporting box and then repeat procedure on other side.

If not using ribbon, place vertical two- or three-inch stems with no leaf side by side at the bottom of stick, to form trunk as in picture. Let dry one hour.

Hang on a string or wire so tree can turn freely. Tie a string around trunk to hold tree steady while spraying paint. (See paint instructions on page 9.) Spray delphinium paint at random intervals. Let dry.

Repeat on other side. Let dry. Spray turquoise the same way. Let dry. Some areas on tree should now have some of both colors in some places and just one color in others. The glitter dust will bring everything together.

Untie tree and place carefully again on supporting box. Spray with glitter glue and add glitter dust quickly at random all over tree. Do this first with delphinium or bright blue, then with turquoise, then with silver dust. If you have decided on a ribbon trunk, attach a doubled loop made of a blue and a green ribbon about three-quarters of an inch wide slightly overlapped into a long doubled loop. Thumb-tack into end grain of wood.

For details in handling coconut palm fronds, see Rainflower, page 44. If this material is substituted for artemisia, the base stick should measure seven inches by one-half inch thick and one inch wide.

6.   ARTEMISIA PUFF TREELET
(Shown in color, Figure 24)

6" wood strip ¾" wide x ½" thick
about 40 short stems of artemisia (small leaved section nearest
    flower head)
blue satin ribbon ⎫
green satin ribbon ⎬ ½" wide, 20" of each
Elmer's Glue-All, glitter glue
floral spray paints: delphinium blue, turquoise, light green,
    silver
glitter dust: blue, silver, turquoise, light green
4" light wire for hanging, or string, or no. 214 screw eye

Alternate for artemisia is untreated polygonum twigs

This treelet is made of the unused parts of the other artemisia tree designs. Even their residual glitter dust can be applied here. The details in the Artemisia Great Tree, page 128, may be useful.

Make hole through stick at top center near edge or place screw eye in end grain at top of stick. Tie a piece of string or fine wire through hole for handling during pasting. This tree must be supported horizontally for the pasting on the second side. Plan a box with thin sides so the puffy first side can rest on the edges of the open box while working the second side.

Let a one-eighth-inch thick column of glue flow down center of stick. It is all right if some of it shifts or drops to the side because this tree trunk stick has branches all around and glue is necessary all around the stick before design is finished. The bottom branch spread in the picture is five inches. Allow for the space used by the trunk or stick and plan the individual low branch placements to be two and one-half inches long.

Let glue set to marshmallow consistency and form trunk at bottom of stick. Glue vertical matching one and one-half-inch long leafless stems side by side for the width of the stick at what will be the bottom of the trunk. Wrap with a temporary wire until dry. Remove wire when placing trunk stems on opposite side of stick and rewire to assure bond while drying. Let dry.

While waiting, glue sides of stick with thin layer of glue. Place a few very short leaf stems to create little pockets for later stick placement. Turn stick and place leaf stems on opposite side in same way as on first side. Add glue to sides of stick and build up tree to match silhouette in picture. Drip more glue in stick area. Puff the placements so the tree has depth and fill in sides, adding glue to stem ends with all placements from now on. When shape is complete let dry one hour.

Support tree on box. Apply silver spray paint from a distance of 10 inches. Spray lightly, shaking can constantly. Turn tree and repeat on other side. Hang tree and spray other colors (optional) a little at a time and at random. Let dry between each application. Let dry before spraying glitter glue.

Place tree flat on box support again for best glitter dust adhesion. Spray glue and apply glitter dust simultaneously one side at a time. Hang tree and apply extra glitter dust if necessary.

Align the green and blue ribbons to form one doubled two-tone ribbon with right sides facing out. Fold in center and tie rope or wire hanging device at top of tree into screw eye. Cut away excess wire after tying ribbon center. Tie ribbon ends in a knot. Leave one-half to one inch of ribbon after knot is made. Cut ribbon ends on slant.

Many small-scale materials can be used for the treelet. Polygonum twigs make a good alternate. Cut the branch joints of polygonum after flowering, to include one-half inch at thickened end of branched joint. Crush thickened end, which is fibrous, with pliers without injuring part where branchlets are attached. Each branchlet has several whiskery parts, each one having a joint that can be cut and pasted.

This frothy design is effective if sprayed with silver and with bright gold. Apply glitter dust, concentrating the glitter on small beach burrs pasted at random throughout the tree.

Two matching size treelets or three of varied small size with height-width ratio kept constant would make a hostess happy.

8 Collages

1. PANEL OF CASSIA AND BIGNONIA

(Shown in color, Figure 26)

A weathered wood strip, 46″ x 2″ x ½″, with a grooved rough surface is a good subject for a linoleum paste base. Do not use linoleum paste for a decoration to hang over a radiator or on a heated wall because it will soften.

The orange halves are turned inside out before drying. This braided pattern of bulky material took 20 minutes to make with a half-inch thick base of linoleum paste. It can be done with glue but takes longer. The materials were spray painted in advance in holiday red, antique gold and silver with a vague hint of pumpkin. After the design was finished it was sprayed very lightly with red and silver.

2. *TWIN PLAQUES*

(Shown in color, Figure 27)

Glycerined akebia branches three to seven inches long and full-blown yucca pods are glued to a seasoned stick 32 inches long, two and one-half inches wide and one-half inch thick. This is a repeat center based pattern. After placements have been made, spray antique gold lightly from a flat angle at both ends and sides of stick. This leaves the dark glycerined akebia with a slight glow and emphasizes the yucca.

After the paint is dry, cover the bare wood at the sides of the design with a diluted half-water and half-Elmer's Glue-All solution and scatter the yucca seeds, brunette on one side and blond on the other, to provide a background. Help them with a tweezer. They should all be flat. The sticks are mounted on three-inch red flocked ribbon pasted to their backs. A wire loop is stapled on the back of one stick so it can be attached to the picture hanger at the end of other stick and can hang intact as one plaque.

The design on the small plaque is an unequal repeat and makes the strip continuous. The ribbons overlap imperceptibly. A canvas picture hanger reinforced with two thumbtacks is pasted at back of ribbon at top. A center wire loop flattened against the side center will allow for possible horizontal hanging.

3. *RUBBER PLANT LEAF PLAQUE*

(Shown in color, Figure 5)

  1 yard of knockout ribbon, gold or silver
  8″ square of wood or plywood ¼″ to ⅜″ thick
  1 split large cone 3″ diameter, stem end or center section
18 glycerin-treated rubber plant leaves
  8 giant hyssop spikes
  1 burdock burr

Elmer's Glue-All, absorbent cotton, scissors, staple gun,
   no. 30 wire
Alternate: glycerin-treated magnolia or rhododendron leaves
   may be substituted for rubber plant

Knockout ribbon is the resultant form after sequins have been
stamped or "knocked out." It is available in several colors: gold is good
with these leaves. As it is easier to cut the plaque to fit the ribbon than
vice versa, check the width of the ribbon carefully. It varies. Then cut

the plaque to a square twice the width of the ribbon. For example a four and one-quarter inch ribbon would call for an eight and one-half inch square plaque.

To measure ribbon wrap the ribbon around the plaque to cover and cut it exactly where it meets. Cut a second strip of ribbon the same size. Line up the selvage edge of one ribbon length with the edge of the plaque and wrap around half of the plaque with neatly cut ends meeting in the center of the plaque. Staple twice at joining area near center of plaque holding firmly so pattern of ribbon meets without overlapping. The stapled area will be covered by the flower. Glue balance of the ribbon joint at outer edges of the plaque. Repeat process with second cut length of ribbon on other half of plaque.

You now have two selvages lined up parallel to each other along the center line of the plaque. Staple the selvages two or three times near the center of the plaque, keeping them exactly parallel and not overlapping. This ribbon covering will be a nice finish whether the design is to be hung on a wall or room divider, or placed on the table. If the plaque is to be hung, an adhesive picture hanger, available in a package in novelty stores, will be a neat device with a little extra glue under the adhesive. This type of hanger can be applied now or later. Paste it flush on a corner edge for a diamond-shaped hanging, or flush with the edge at a center point for a square hanging.

Put a large blob of glue in the center of the plaque to hold the cone in which the leaves for the flower will be placed. Let set while you wire the cone. Wiring is not necessary if you plan to use the plaque on a flat surface. In this case, place cone on glue in center of plaque with petals turned upward.

To wire cone, wind a 10-inch length of no. 30 wire one and one-half times around the base of the cone so the wires extend at opposite sides of cone. Repeat with another equal length of wire inserted to extend at opposite sides from the first wire. Bend all four wires back toward center of flower in a U shape and staple to plaque at the rounded end of each wire. (See page 38 for cone method.) Press onto glue, let set 15 minutes.

Dribble glue generously around core of cone and outward on cone petal. Let set while you cut the heavy veined stem ends off the leaves. Dab glue on both sides of stem ends of leaves and poke between the petals of the cone, starting at the base of the cone and making opposite placements each time to create a realistic blossom form. If you have various size leaves the larger leaves should be placed at the bottom of the cone and the smaller ones toward the top.

Placements are best alternated with each successive row so no leaf is directly on top of the leaf in the row below. Glue hyssop spikes around the center of flower as shown in the picture and glue the burdock burr in center of cone to complete.

4. *FISHTAIL PALM MEDALLION*

(Shown in color, Figure 25)

2   large fishtail palm fronds
1   stem end split of a large southern pine cone with three rows
        of petals
2–8″ no. 30 wires for attaching cone to ribbon
        about 4′ of 3″ burlap ribbon
        Elmer's Glue-All
        Derusto spray paint
        Floral spray paint: silver, bright red

The cone is wired between the two petal rows nearest cut end with two separate eight-inch no. 30 wires each twisted once at opposite sides of cone. This wire is threaded through burlap ribbon and back through the ribbon to tie under cone. Face stem end forward so it will not scratch hanging surface.

Cut sections of fishtail palm jagged leaf edges along leaf veins. Drench cone core with glue between both rows of cone petals. Cut three to five inch sections of fishtail palm jagged leaf tips. They are a one-sided fan shape. Paste largest forms in bottom row, making matching size opposite placements each time. Add more glue in cone core area only, so leaf tips are free and place petals slightly smaller all around, again making opposite placements but slightly shorter. Repeat procedure in next row, opposite and shorter, and if the medallion looks too flat, put in an additional row adding paste with each leaf tip. Fluorescent red and floral paint spray of silver and bright gold are alternated. Ribbon is looped down over front with a double roll and up over bottom the same way. A piece of fine wire or thread holds the rolled loop across width of ribbon.

5. CURTAIN RAISER SACHET

A rosette of sea grape leaves with tassel-like sensitive fern trim is made on an oval Masonite scrap a quarter inch wide and five inches long. If it is to be used for a tieback, drill holes in plaque and leave string to be removed at end of work and replaced with a cord. A prepasted canvas picture hanger added at the back with extra glue will accommodate other hanging needs. With Elmer's Glue-All paste scotch pine cone center to Masonite and insert with glycerined sea grape leaves with large leaves at bottom and small ones toward center top. Let dry twenty minutes.

The final large petal placements are tucked outside under the bottom of the cone and will be supported only by the linoleum paste. Spray with gold'n'pearl floral paint spray over a light coat of Christmas red. Place wisps of dried lavender or rose geranium in open pods with a generous dab of glue. These will lose their scent if painted.

This is interesting in several sizes as an innovation in drape tie-backs for the holidays as well as a table accessory or wall plaque.

6. *JACARANDA AND PERSIMMON*

These small shapes suggest nesting birds; the dried lavender tucked into the jacaranda could be a ruffled feather. The composition is interesting done in varied sizes of one, two, or three pods and a persimmon calyx. Glue to quarter inch Masonite ovals about 6 by 2 inches. Hang individually in groups on nylon thread. Spray gold'n'pearl floral paint over light blue *before* the lavender is inserted with glue.

7. *PIGNON PORCUPINE WITH TASSEL*

(Shown in color, Figure 24)

1–2″ Styrofoam ball
    about 40 pignon cone petals or two medium pignon cones
    about 2 yards of red yarn
    Elmer's Glue-All
    a marking needle (open end eye) or a 5″ strong needle as used in
      upholstery, or a long nail to drive through ball for hanger

    Alternate for cone petals: peony seed pods and rose hips

A strong needle or long nail can be driven down through the center of a Styrofoam ball in several different ways. To get it centered, pencil a small cross on the top. Place ball in a shallow cup or tin can to hold it firm with cross in exact center of top. Drive nail straight down through center of crossed lines and you will probably have it just right. This ball is completely covered with cone petals when finished so if you don't hit the target the first time, try again.

A needle with an open end eye can be fitted with a loop of yarn. A double length of 14-inch yarn should now be pulled through center of ball. This leaves a nine-inch loop of yarn above the ball and two three-inch ends coming out bottom end of ball.

Cut eight six-inch lengths of yarn. Tie together in the center and double at tie point. Wrap five or six times with yarn around looped double point. Knot, and tie to ends of yarn extending from bottom of ball. Tie the tassel by pulling one of the two ends of the doubled yarn through the tassel loop. Mask the tassel and top string with tissue or paper towel. Set ball on a small can or glass so tassel does not get too abused and cover surface of ball not resting in glass with a generous application of glue. Pare petals from cones with a knife. Carefully place cone petals close to the tip form of the petal, dipping each placement in glue before sticking in the Styrofoam ball. Let placements dry one half-hour.

Poke a firm wire into area where long yarn extends from ball. It can serve as a stem to place in a bottle to relieve stress while petals are now placed in bottom section of ball. Apply glue to this section generously. Let set five minutes. Place petals to cover, let dry.

This very simple tiny form is made with handsome materials and does not need to be spray painted.

Kissing balls are meant for mistletoe. Tuck some in area of tassel loop.

8. STEPHANANDRA KISSING BALL

(Shown in color, Figure 24)

60 to 100 glycerined stephanandra leaves
1–3″ Styrofoam ball
    Elmer's Glue-All, a Q-tip, nylon thread
    a marking needle (open eye) or strong wire for inserting
       hanging wire
    floral spray paints: silver, bright gold
    glitter dust: silver, bright blue, bright green
⅜″ wide satin ribbon, blue and green, 16″ long

> *Alternate:* andromeda or honeysuckle have a different leaf
>   pattern but form a pretty ball. The cone petals of the
>   sugar pine are dramatic used with a definite horizontal or
>   spiraled pattern. See end note.

To insert hanging wire in center of ball set Styrofoam ball on a water glass or small can. Bear down on ball and twist to indent rim on Styrofoam. Mark a small cross on ball at top center. Invert ball and twist to indent rim mark on ball again. Make large cross on top of ball by drawing two intersecting lines from rim to rim and mark center at intersection. Repeat intersecting mark on bottom of ball.

With ball set on glass to fit one of the rim marks, drive hole with heavy needle or wire halfway through ball at center. Invert ball and insert needle at center mark again. You will probably connect. It helps to line path of needle with a vertical wall board or door casing to keep the path straight. When needle goes through, leave in place, thread eye with ten inches of doubled fine wire or string. Knot ends of string and pull through ball. Slip doubled end out of needle or cut at center and tie. This end should now be pulled back almost flush with ball. Insert a small stick temporarily in this end between ball and wire so you can get in to tie ribbon at finishing stage. This will be the bottom of the ball. Pull knot end tight and knot again at top end of ball. Invert ball on glass and cover liberally with glue. Let set ten minutes. The bottom end is now facing up.

Cut stems from leaves. Apply leaves in rings around ball from here down with tip points of petals pointing in toward center mark on ball. Paste the first leaves entirely. After that, place the next row to overlap and paste firmly but only at the stem end leaving the tip of leaf free to curl slightly. Continue going around ball placing one row at a time until you have covered the first half of the ball. Invert ball and cover rest of ball with glue. Let set. Continue pasting petals in same direction as the previous pastings until complete with well-matched petals at top center. Let hang free to dry for a half-hour after wiping excess glue from leaves. A Q-tip is handy for this.

Check to see all placements are firm. The ball should have kept its round shape with the tiny tips of the leaf slightly curled away from the ball. If the tips seem to extend too much and have too shaggy an effect, slip ball, top end first, into a plastic bag and pull plastic tight at top end and let set that way for an hour. It will control the leaves easily and is faster than poking.

When thoroughly dry, spray lightly first with silver paint, then lightly with bright gold. Dilute a tablespoon of Elmer's Glue-All with water, half and half. Pull cotton from one end of Q-tip to use as a dabber and dab every third or fourth leaf tip with glue. Do half the ball at a time. Sprinkle mixed glitter dust over a box, collect fallout. After glitter dust has set in about five minutes invert the ball and glue tips of leaves on the other half of the ball. Sprinkle glitter and let dry.

Double the ribbons so right side is out. Make a soft loop of a third of the doubled ribbon. Twist in center of loop with a small piece of wire to form a two-inch loop with a short end and a long end. Pry stick out of bottom of ball and tie loop at twist area to the centering wire or string. To make firm, check top twist or knot of wire by giving one extra turn. This makes a loop for a hanging device. Nylon thread is the nicest. Attach mistletoe to ribbon loop.

Note: For spiraled pattern of cone petals make a diagonal placement of one row of petals from two inches at the right of center top to two inches at the left of center bottom. Apply glue in broad lines to pattern the placements. Make next row about two inches away keeping parallel to first line. Fill in at sides of each spiral line, keeping spiral by doing a parallel line each time.

9. *HONESTY AND AKEBIA CANDLE HOLDER*

18   hemlock cones
18   honesty petals
36   glycerin-treated akebia leaves (*alternate:* white spruce cones,
        all split forms, leucothoe or andromeda leaves)
1–4″ Styrofoam ball
    3″ round of strong paper or flocked ribbon to cover base of ball
1   white taper 12″ to 16″ tall
     plastic coffee can cover
     hollow metal tube 1½″ in diameter and about 4″ long
     gold'n'pearl floral spray paint
     glue, small knife
     plaster of Paris (One cup of dry plaster with water added to form
        a whipped cream consistency. This sets immediately so do not
        mix until you are ready to use.)

Slice an end about two and one-half inches in diameter from Styrofoam ball. Discard the circle. The ball now has a flat base of two and one-half inches. Measure and cut a strong paper or ribbon to cover this base for a smooth protective finish and set aside.

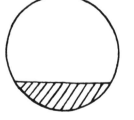

Push the metal tube straight down into the center of the ball and pull out or push all the way through the ball, removing the tube and a core of Styrofoam approximately one and one-half inches in diameter. Set ball on plastic coffee can cover for next step. Fill the hollowed-out space with the plaster mixture to within a half inch of the top of the ball and place the candle firmly down into the wet plaster. Line the candle up with some vertical wall line and hold in place a minute or so until you feel it is supported by the drying plaster. Wipe off

excess plaster around candle gently before it dries. Let set 10 minutes.

Put dime-size drops of glue around the top quarter of the ball to within a quarter inch of the candle hole. Place three whole hemlock cones, blossom end up and stem end in the glue in a triangular pattern one and one-half inches away from candle, facing up and away. Fill in the remaining space on the top quarter of the ball with tips and bottoms of split hemlock cones. Leave a quarter inch rim around candle to assure its easy removal.

Slide knife carefully between base of ball and plastic coffee lid where plaster may have adhered to lid, loosen completely and prop ball on a coffee tin or sturdy inverted glass which will act as a turntable. This also will enable you to see the line of akebia leaves at the base of the ball to make sure they do not hang over the base or touch the table. Apply glue from the base of the ball up to the hemlock cones on the side that faces you. Starting at the base of the ball, place the akebia leaves, stem end up, in a row along the bottom so they overlap enough to cover. Glue leaves only at first half inch of stem end so the dimpled tip of leaf hangs free of the Styrofoam. Continue with the next row, placing the tip of the leaves in this row to overlap the stem ends of the row below and repeat until you join the line of the hemlock cones.

Conceal the stem ends at this joining point by tucking them under the edges of the cones. Working half the ball at a time keeps the glue soft enough to allow for adjustments. Repeat the procedure on the other side of the ball.

Your work may have been so precise that you do not need to use any spray paint and this is a very pretty design in its natural color. If you do want to spray it with gold'n'pearl floral paint as in the picture, this should be done now before placing the honesty petals in the cones.

To spray: Mask the candle with tissue paper (which is adequate to protect it and will not bruise it) or remove it by twisting it gently up and out and spray ball with gold'n'pearl floral spray paint as directed on page 9.

When paint is dry, remove ball from glass. Whisk away any particles that may have stuck to the bottom of the ball to prepare for the finishing. The ribbon or paper covering which you have cut and set aside will go on smoothly. Coat bottom of ball with adequate amount of glue, apply finishing circle of ribbon or paper, and set firmly down on the cleaned plastic coffee can lid to dry. If any excess glue should come through it will be easy to pry the ball off the plastic lid when it is dry.

While it is drying, dab glue between the petals of the whole hemlock cones where the honesty petals will be inserted to create the flower form.

Cut stems from the honesty petals to allow deep placement within the hemlock cone. Take care not to cut into the frame of the honesty petal as that would destroy its shape. See sketch, page 36.

To make an open flower, place petals near base of cone, pointing outward. To make a bud, place petals around top pointing upward. Some honesty petals are curved. You will see how to utilize this curve to make either the open or the bud form. All the petals in each flower should curl the same way—all outward or all inward. This design has two open flowers and one bud.

Dab glue gently on end of petal to be poked into cone one at a time as the glue quickly softens the petal and prevents it from being easily placed. Make opposite placements each time to achieve a natural looking blossom form.

This design can be rescaled to a miniature size (two and one-half or three inch Styrofoam ball) to be used singly or in groups. All materials should be reduced in scale, including the candle, and a single honesty flower should replace the three flower forms in the above design. Care must be taken to have the candle tall enough to burn at least one hour and be well balanced in the plaster of Paris core.

10. *PETALED CANDLE HOLDERS*
(Shown in color, Figure 28)

petals from one cone of digger pine; petals from two pignon cones

The digger pine cone petals with spread heavy points and the large petals of the pignon pine cone are clipped neatly at the stem end and pasted with glue or linoleum paste around a taper fitted into a can filled with plaster of Paris. The wax taper is easily supported by the weight of the plaster. It could hold a full width, very tall candle. The drip will shine the petals and cannot splatter on a table top. The candles sit in the plaster of Paris as described in the previous design. The burlap ribbon is cut exactly to width of can and joined in a flat vertical one-inch loop with paste to hold it. Pin several places at loop or bind tightly with wide paper strip while drying. Mask ribbon before proceeding. Apply a good layer of linoleum paste on top of plaster of Paris. Paste petals.

Appendix

LIST OF MATERIALS USED BY

ROXBURY-BRIDGEWATER GARDEN CLUB

Cones: all kinds, especially Norway spruce, white, red, scotch pine, and hemlock

Small nut forms

Seed Pods: need no treatment

abutilon	hyssop	sweet pea
acorns	iris (any)	tansy
alder	leucothoe	teasel
andromeda	lily and lilium	trumpet vine
artemisia	lunaria (honesty,	tulip tree
beech	silver dollar)	witch hazel
burdock	magnolia	yarrow
bur-reed	mallow	yucca
catalpa	maple	
Chinese lantern	martinia	*Tropical*
clematis	milkweed	
cucumber (wild)	okra	agave
datura (angel trumpet)	peony	jacaranda
evening primrose	poppy	lipstick
gum (green)	rhododendron	palm (any)
hosta	sensitive fern	sandalwood

Dried Stalks: cut while green — do not need glycerin

Indian cup	*Tropical*
mustard	
polygonum	bamboo
plume poppy	palm (any kind)
radish	sea grape
scotch broom	
(can also be glycerined)	

Plumes:

miscanthus
pampas
sea oats

Berry Forms:

bayberry	pokeweed
cabbage palm	privet
euonymus	rose hips (large)
Florida holly	

Leaves:

Oak leaves are durable without treatment
Glycerin the following: Materials should be at mature growth

akebia	physostegia
andromeda	rhododendron
bay	smilax
beech	stephanandra
coltsfoot	sweet fern
eucalyptus (all kinds)	sycamore
viburnum (all kinds)	
holly	*Tropical*
honeysuckle	
ivy (evergreen)	dracaena
leucothöe	rubber plant
mulberry	sea grape
mullein	strelitzia

To glycerin: Place fresh cut stem end or branch not over one foot long in solution of one-third glycerin and two-thirds water. Maintain two-inch liquid level in base of container by adding water: conditioning time one to three weeks according to size of stem end or branch. When removing from container be sure to keep leaves free of solution. Leaves may be used separately or left on branch.

Fruit and Vegetable Forms

banana skins
lemons
limes
oranges
eggplant and persimmon stem ends (calyx)
okra (whole)
squash (small round or oval)

Preparation: lemons, limes, oranges; cut in half as for squeezing, turn skin inside out, remove pulp, and pierce hole on both sides of center about one-half inch apart with large needle. Let inverted skins dry slowly.

Bananas: peel lengthwise, carefully scrape out pulp and let skin strips dry slowly. For quick conditioning; bake skins in 200 degree oven for twenty minutes. Large or small banana peels make interesting leaf forms when properly conditioned.

Eggplant and persimmon stem ends; pierce both sides of center as close as possible while soft. Let dry slowly.

Okra (whole); pierce on both sides of stem while soft, draw thread through holes and tie. Let dry slowly.

Squash; cut in half using stem and opposite end of stem half as centers. Place open part on baking tin and make at 325 for twenty minutes or until pulp is edible. For half with center stem; pierce both sides of stem as close as possible while soft. For the half without stem; pierce holes same as above, in same area. Use large needle.

Note: after baking, carefully remove pulp from squash halves.

GARDEN LIBRARY
PLANTING FIELDS ARBORETUM

SB
449.3   Metzler, Rejean.
.D7
M47   Forever flowers.

DATE DUE			

LIBRARY
PLANTING FIELDS FOUNDATION